Ruining Christmas—Rediscovering Jesus

Merry Christmas!

Ruining Christmas—Rediscovering Jesus

Carl N. Toney

CASCADE *Books* • Eugene, Oregon

RUINING CHRISTMAS—REDISCOVERING JESUS

Cascade Books
An Imprint of Wipf and Stock Publishers
199 W. 8th Ave., Suite 3
Eugene, OR 97401

www.wipfandstock.com

PAPERBACK ISBN: 978-1-7252-9526-1
HARDCOVER ISBN: 978-1-7252-9525-4
EBOOK ISBN: 978-1-7252-9527-8

Cataloguing-in-Publication data:

Names: Toney, Carl N., author.

Title: Ruining Christmas—Rediscovering Jesus / by Carl N. Toney.

Description: Eugene, OR: Cascade Books, 2021 | Includes bibliographical references and index.

Identifiers: ISBN 978-1-7252-9526-1 (paperback) | ISBN 978-1-7252-9525-4 (hardcover) | ISBN 978-1-7252-9527-8 (ebook)

Subjects: LCSH: Jesus Christ—Nativity. | Christmas.

Classification: BT315.2 T66 2021 (print) | BT315.2 (ebook)

08/17/21

For Larry and Teena Toney

Contents

Acknowledgments

Thanks to everyone who has wished me a "Merry Christmas" over the years. Thanks to my parents, Larry and Teena Toney, who raised me to love Christmas, and thanks to my sister, Trisha, who got the other half of the presents. Thanks to my wife, Lisa, and my kids, Zoe, Gus, Pax, and Eden, and our dog, Apricot, who have helped create new Christmas memories and traditions. Thanks to my extended family including Trisha, John, Kristina, Bob, Lenora, Paul, Jessica, Lindsey, Andy, Jack, Charlotte, Kristin, Jenna, Nick, Hannah and Ellie, James, Julie, Ty, and Lauren. I continue to be grateful for my friends, Drs. Katy and Kevin Lines, Laura and Dr. Jane B. Wilgus, Dr. David Creech, Drs. Jen and Dave Downs, Dr. Fay Ellwood and Dr. Pat Horn, Wendy and Dr. Curtis Holtzen, Sarah and Dr. Phil Towne, Dr. Kelly Dagley, Linda and Dr. Joe Grana, Elaine and Dr. Tim Dally, Sarah and Dr. Matt Jenson, Dr. Larisa Levicheva Joseph and Dr. Abson Joseph, Dr. Brannon Hancock, Christina and Jarrett LeMaster, Camille and Eric Waage, Amy and Andy Rosdil, Sarah and Ryan Trobaugh, Jen and Mark Bryan, Ali and Kiley Wallace, Jenny and Luke Bayon, Shane Drake, Kimberly and Glenn Gunderson, and Miyia and Gene Hawkins, and everyone in Coram Deo.

Carl N. Toney
Hope International University
Fullerton, CA
Christmas 2020

Abbreviations

For abbreviations of biblical books, ancient sources, journals, commentaries, and monograph series, please consult *The SBL Handbook of Style,* second edition.

Introduction: Ruining Christmas—
Rediscovering Jesus

H ave you ever complained about Christmas being "ruined"? I know I
have.

We can come up with all sorts of ways we feel the holiday has been
ruined. Maybe we got the wrong gift. Maybe all the gift giving and Christmas sales feel too commercialized. Maybe we're spending the holiday
alone or away from loved ones. Or maybe we wish that we could get away
from our loved ones. Maybe we wish churches would do more to celebrate
Christmas. Or maybe we wish they would do less. Maybe Christmas
feels too traditional. Or maybe it doesn't feel traditional enough. Maybe
Christmas feels too much like a religion. Or maybe we just don't buy that
it's all about a relationship.

We can probably all come up with reasons why Christmas can feel
ruined. So are there ways that we can learn from the times that Christmas
has been ruined? Can we rediscover Jesus when Christmas is ruined? Alternatively, does ruining Christmas always have to be a bad thing? What if

there are ways that we are supposed to ruin Christmas? What if we are able to ruin Christmas in order to rediscover Jesus?

Breaking Stuff

Unfortunately, stories can be ruined through repetition and familiarity. Stories can become stale because we know them so well. They can become boring. We can lose interest in the story. For some of us, Christmas has been ruined because of how ordinary it has become.

If this is your experience, then maybe this book can rejuvenate those ruined memories. Maybe it can give you fresh eyes and ears to rediscover Jesus.

For others of us, Christmas has lost its magic. When we were children, we were enamored by the Christmas stories. We were excited by the traditions and by the presents. We sat with unquestioning ears. We listened with wonder to the story of the miraculous birth of Jesus.

Then we grew up.

We began to question the plausibility of Mary being pregnant by any other means than by a man. We started sifting the Bible for the historical details of Jesus's birth. We attempted to winnow the kernel of history from the chaff of the miraculous or the mythical.[1] Just as we stopped believing in Santa Claus, so we began to stop believing in Jesus.

If this is you, then maybe we can rediscover our imaginations together. Maybe we can gather together the wood of our broken mangers, and this book can offer a spark to rekindle our dreams.

For still others of us, Christmas has been ruined by the spectacle of it all. We've floundered upon the special effects, the live animals, and the climate-controlled events. Maybe we've become jaded by our churches portraying the Holy Family in a manner that looks like us. Maybe we're tired of seeing a baby Jesus who is White, Black, Asian, Hispanic, or so forth. Instead, we want to see a little Jewish baby.

If you can identify with this, then maybe this book can be a call for simplicity. Maybe this book can help us to rediscover a poor, Jewish family that welcomed their son into the world on that first Christmas night.

---

1. One of the best studies on the birth stories of Jesus remains Brown, *Birth of the Messiah*.

Spoilers Ahead

Some things are ruined when we know the ending. In today's internet age full of Google searches, I have to admit that one of my pet peeves involves glancing through the sports and entertainment sections of the news because my search engine's headlines often reveal the game's final score or the movie's crucial plot twist.

Maybe we feel like all the drama of Christmas has been ruined because we already know the end of the story. We are not surprised by Mary's pregnancy . . . because the Bible tells us that the child comes from the Holy Spirit. We know that Joseph won't divorce her . . . because he will have a dream that tells him everything's fine. There is no amazement when the angels appear to the shepherds . . . because they seem to be appearing to everyone. We're not surprised when the magi find Jesus . . . because we know that they can follow a star. We don't feel the threat of Herod seeking to kill baby Jesus . . . because we know that he'll escape.

Has Christmas been ruined for you because there are no more spoilers? Maybe this book will reveal a few surprises that can help recapture our wonder when we read the Christmas story.

Birthday Cake

Other things are enjoyed more when we know the outcome, and they're not ruined. Sometimes we need consistency in our lives. Every year my wife bakes my favorite chocolate cake for my birthday. Take a moment to think about your favorite cake. Then multiply that level of deliciousness by a thousand.

This cake is amazing. Each bite simply melts in your mouth because chocolate pudding has been folded into the batter. Real chocolate chips please your pallet because they are melted and mixed in for a solid foundation of a rich flavor. Then, even more chocolate chips are added, making little chocolate treasures for your tongue to discover. Finally, each bite is complemented by the cream cheese frosting that enfolds every slice.

But the deliciousness of this cake isn't just about the flavor. It also fills me with nostalgic memories from my childhood because this is the same recipe that my mom used to make. I look forward to my cake each year because I already know what it will taste like. The smells of freshly baked cake get me excited for my upcoming birthday celebration and cause me to remember all the good times from past birthdays.

For the Christmas story, we already know how it begins and ends. After all, since the time of Mary and Joseph, it's been a story that's been told for over two thousand years. Like my chocolate cake, there are no surprises because we already know the recipe. In fact, by following the recipe, we ensure that our cake isn't ruined.

Just as a good cake relies upon the right amount of flour, sugar, and eggs, so we enjoy the Christmas story when we include Mary, Joseph, and Jesus along with all the other complementing spices from the shepherds to the magi. It is precisely because we've followed the recipes of the Christmas story that it is not ruined, and we can enjoy it every time. This certainty of Christmas can give us hope, particularly when we experience times of uncertainty.

The Year Christmas Was Canceled

Sometimes Christmas feels ruined for more serious reasons. Would Christmas be ruined if it was canceled? In Dr. Seuss's *How the Grinch Stole Christmas!* the Grinch plots to ruin Christmas by stealing all the presents of Whoville. However, much to the Grinch's surprise, the Whos are unfazed by his theft and begin to cheerfully sing. From this, he learns that the holiday has a deeper meaning, and he ends up returning all the gifts.

Unfortunately, the cancellation of Christmas moved from fiction to reality for many of us when the coronavirus pandemic shut down the world in 2020. In many parts of the world, churches had to grapple with how to celebrate Christmas, or even if they should celebrate Christmas. Shops, restaurants, and businesses dramatically altered their services, and many had to close during the season.

Families were forced to decide if they would gather together for Christmas. The loss of jobs and homes made Christmas look still different for others. For those who caught the coronavirus, Christmas meant spending Christmas in isolation or in the hospital. Even worse, other families felt the pain of loved ones dying from the virus.

Did you feel like Christmas was ruined in 2020? All the disruptions and tragedies forced individuals, families, and society to rethink priorities during the Christmas season. When Christmas is ruined, we have to decide what are the essential aspects of Christmas.

Have we ever thought about the ways the first Christmas was ruined for Jesus's family? For example, how were their lives being disrupted by the Roman census? Maybe Jesus can relate to our pain and offer comfort.

While some of us may not have experienced a loss in 2020, we can think of other years where we've lost a loved one, and we face Christmas with a hole in our hearts. We can think of a time where we lost a job and wondered how we would survive. Maybe our family has been broken by a divorce or another tragedy. Maybe our Christmas memories are full of arguments, feeling alone, depressed, hungry, unloved, or stressed. Maybe some other painful memories have ruined Christmas.

Sometimes when life is ruined, all that we can hope for is to rediscover Jesus. For those of us who have faced a ruined Christmas, maybe this book can help us to rediscover Jesus.

When It's Good to Ruin Things

However, we can also think more positively about ruining Christmas. Some things are meant to be ruined. When was the last time you played a board game? Every game begins with the ruins of the previous game that have been put back in the box.

At the beginning of each game, the first thing that you must do is set up the game. This can be something as simple as a game like Chutes and Ladders where you get out the board and spinner and then place the players' markers on the start position. Or it can become increasingly complex from games like Monopoly to German board games like Settlers of Catan.

We can discover hours of fun when we play board games as long as we are willing to reset the board at the end of each game. It's certainly no fun having a board turned over in the middle of a game. It's also not much fun if we lose every time we play. But when the game is over, we reset the board in order to play again.

Maybe we feel like we've played the Christmas game to its very end. Maybe we feel like we've played the game of our lives to the end. Maybe we already know who the winners and losers are. Maybe it's time for us to reset the board. Can we look at Christmas differently? Can we look at ourselves differently? Can we look at life differently?

Maybe this book can be our chance to ruin the board before we start the game anew. With a reset board comes hope and possibility. Maybe we can learn how to win the game.

Creatures of Habit

There are other things that we're better-off ruining. Do you have any bad habits that you'd like to get rid of? I bite my nails. Habits get formed when we think or do something over and over. We may try to cultivate "good" habits like improving our diet and exercise. Alternatively, we may discourage "bad" habits like smoking or swearing. While we're not always successful in choosing good habits over bad ones, we tend to have a built-in sense that we should be cultivating good habits and ruining our bad ones.

Sometimes we learn good habits by getting rid of bad habits. Maybe you're trying to improve your diet by eating more vegetables and less meat. Maybe you're trying to change what time you go to bed at night. Maybe you're trying to improve your attitude by focusing on positive things.

Other times, we realize that we can't make these improvements on our own, so sometimes we enlist an expert's help. If you wanted to improve your golf swing, you might hire a coach. If you want to be a better cook, you might take a class or hire a chef. If you wanted to learn to fix a car, you might get advice from a mechanic.

We've all formed habits for how we read our Bibles. When we read the Bible on our own, it's easy to fall back on how we've been taught to read. It's also possible to improve our understanding of the stories of Scripture through practice. But sometimes, it can be helpful to enlist the help of a professional. In fact, if you've ever sat through a Christmas sermon, you've experienced what that means to get an expert's help at understanding Scripture. But you've probably also discovered that there is a whole range in these experts' abilities and knowledge.

As we think about ruining Christmas, we need to ask ourselves if we've picked up any bad habits over time. When reading the Christmas stories, do we skip the "boring" parts like Jesus's genealogy? Maybe we jump past the violent parts like Herod killing the infants. Do we fixate upon baby Jesus in the manger while ignoring the experiences of Mary and Joseph? Have we ever blurred the stories found in Matthew and Luke? Or do we add extra cast members like Joseph and Mary's donkey?

It's possible that we need to ruin a few of our bad habits that have formed while reading the Christmas story. We want to break down some of our less helpful understandings of Christmas in order to come away with stronger, healthier habits for reading the Christmas story. Perhaps, through a better understanding of Christmas, we can even be transformed into better and healthier versions of ourselves.

Driving Down the Wrong Side of the Road

Think about when you learned to drive. We had to learn all sorts of routines. With the advent of seat belt laws, we were taught to put on our seat belts before starting the car. We also learned to put our foot on the brake when starting the ignition. While driving, we learned to look far enough down the road to drive in the center of our lanes. We also developed a pattern of turning on our turn signals and looking before changing lanes.

We can grow comfortable and confident in our routines. However, even normally good routines can become dangerous when circumstances change, but we don't change. We are taught to drive on the right side of the road in the United States. But if you go to another country like Eswatini (formerly Swaziland), you must learn to drive on the left side of the road. If you rely on your ingrained routines, someone might end up hurt, or worse.

Now, most of us may not be traveling to Eswatini anytime soon. Still, maybe my next illustration can serve as a public safety announcement. When I learned to drive, I was taught to put my hands at the ten o'clock and two o'clock positions of the steering wheel. But nowadays, drivers learn to put their hands at nine and three. Why? What changed?

Airbags.

It turns out that if you keep your hands at the old driving positions, then you risk punching yourself in the face or breaking a wrist if you get into a car accident. To help protect drivers from airbags, new drivers are taught to put their hands at nine and three.

Sometimes even knowledge that was good and useful during an earlier point in our lives can become unhelpful or even dangerous if we're not aware of how our life circumstances have changed. Could it be that we've been taught some good but faulty information about Christmas? Are we open to the possibility of letting go of some of our past routines? Is it possible to learn to read Bible stories in a better way? Can we allow ourselves to ruin some traditions that we have held as dear so that we are open to new insights from these stories?

Holiday Decorations

I would imagine that most of us don't keep our Christmas decorations up all year long. Instead, we put them away so we can recreate Christmas each year. I love Christmas, and it's always tempting to keep the house decorated. However, I still put my ornaments away because my friends would look at me strangely if they came over in the middle of July and saw my fake Christmas tree set up in the middle of my living room.

Part of what makes each holiday special is that we take the time to intentionally celebrate that one moment for a short time each year. Christmas, Easter, Thanksgiving, and the Fourth of July—these are all holidays that my family loves to gather together and celebrate. But each of these is only celebrated once a year.

While Christmas can feel a bit ruined at the end of each holiday season as we take down our decorations, we also can get excited for the next Christmas. For the Christmas story, we can find joy in the completed picture. Still, enjoyment is also found in the process of recreating the Christmas story each year in fresh ways.

Getting Out the Legos

One of my favorite toys as a kid was Legos. Legos are amazing because you can build almost anything that your imagination allows. But when you buy a Lego set, it is usually designed to build a specific toy.

Maybe I wanted to build a car, a truck, a space shuttle, or the Millennium Falcon. Then, I would buy that set and build the toy. After opening the box, I would dump out all the pieces and find the instructions. What's incredible about Legos is that you start with what appears to be a random pile of pieces. But after following the step-by-step instructions, you end up building your own new toy.

Sometimes I would build such amazing toys that I didn't want ever to destroy them. This was especially true for bigger, more complex sets. But the problem was that if I never destroyed my toys, then I wouldn't have the chance to enjoy the process of making something new.

If you've ever watched the *Lego Movie*, then you know that this is one of the movie's basic premises. The heroes are "master builders" who can make creations out of anything. At the same time, the villains want to do whatever they can to keep things the same, even if it means permanently gluing pieces together.

When it comes to reading the Bible, we tend to approach the Christmas story like the step-by-step instructions of a Lego set. The first time we read the Christmas story, we're excited! We follow the instructions given to us by our churches, our families, and our communities to build our stable and manger. We include all the key characters of Mary, Joseph, and Jesus. We add shepherds and sheep. We play with our magi and star. We may even include our villains like King Herod. After following the instructions, we have a sense of satisfaction that we have put all the right pieces in their proper places.

Like my Lego creations, many of the Christmas stories and traditions that we've built can give us hours of enjoyment. We may have done a great job following the instructions we were given. The Bible gives us our basic building blocks for understanding the Christmas story. But, unlike my Legos, we don't have just one set of instructions for creating our Christmas traditions. We can find enjoyment as we learn about Christmas traditions from our churches, families, and communities. We also can find joy in learning new traditions from other churches, families, and cultures.

The joy of Legos isn't just building the right set and putting it up on our shelves. The joy of Legos is found in the process of building and rebuilding new creations. The joy of Legos is sharing with others our creations. The joy of Legos is learning from others how to make even more incredible creations. Like my Legos, we are invited each Christmas season to create something new. What if we could take apart our Christmas Lego set and make an even more spectacular nativity story?

When it comes to the Christmas story, I want each of us to become "master builders." The first step is to tear apart our creations and start again. Of course, at any time we can always follow our old instructions and re-build our original creations. I hope that these next few pages will give us a chance to "ruin" Christmas in order to build it anew. My hope is that we are able to find Jesus as we play with these stories.

If you are someone who feels like Christmas has been ruined, this book is for you. If you are someone who feels like Christmas needs a little bit of ruining, this book is for you. Let's dismantle some of our stories about Christmas so that we can look afresh upon the Christmas story and build something new. For others of us, these rebuilt stories may look very familiar to what we've built before, but we discover that enjoyment is found in the process of building and telling these stories.

Let's ruin Christmas and rediscover Jesus!

Reflection Questions

1. What are some of your favorite things about the Christmas season? Do you have any special Christmas family traditions? Are there things you don't look forward to about Christmas?

2. If you were to tell someone the Christmas story, what are the essential parts to the story?

3. What are your favorite parts of the Christmas story? Do you have any parts of the Christmas story that you skip over? Are there any parts of the Christmas story that you struggle with?

4. Have you ever read a book, heard a sermon, watched a movie, listened to a song, and so forth that made the Christmas story come alive or become more meaningful for you?

5. What are some of your good habits? Do you have any good habits when it comes to reading the Bible?

6. What are some of your bad habits? Are there any Bible reading habits that you'd like to improve or change?

7. Do you prefer to "follow the instructions" or "be creative" when doing something new (maybe it's assembling a piece of furniture, cooking, fixing something, etc.)? What's the relationship between "following the instructions" and "being creative" for reading, understanding, and applying Bible stories?

8. How do you feel about the idea of ruining Christmas so that we can rediscover Jesus?

Activity: Scripture Reading

Each chapter will conclude with an activity to help enrichen our understanding of the Christmas story. We'll begin by reflecting upon the Christmas story in Luke. Ignatius of Loyola taught an approach to reading Scripture that can help bring biblical stories to life using our imaginations.

Read Luke 2:1–7. Create the scene in your imagination of what this would have been like. Using your five senses, what do you see (such as the setting and people), hear, smell, taste, and feel? Next, insert yourself into this scene. Which character are you? Where do you belong? How do you feel? Talk to characters in the story? Where is Jesus? How is he looking at you? Do you hear God speaking a specific word for you? Pray and reflect upon your experience.

2

Ruining the Birthday Party— Rediscovering the Celebration

I was born in 1975, the same year that *Jaws* was released. I learned about the date of my birthday from the parties that my parents threw for me as a kid. As I got older, I learned to mark my calendar and look forward to my birthday each year. At least six months before my birthday, I would begin making my wish list, asking my parents for all my favorite toys.

Even during those times when my birthday fell on a weekday, but we had the party on the weekend, I still knew the date of my real birthday. In high school, I would celebrate by going to the local Denny's to get my free meal—no matter which day of the week my birthday occurred.

I've never doubted the date that I was born, and my birth certificate easily confirms it. Anyone who wants to check my age can now look at my driver's license. Further, my parents have photos of me in the hospital that have the date written on them.

Because I know the date of my birth, it's easy to figure out how old I am. Knowing my age was important as I passed certain milestones in American culture. For example, as a five-year-old, I went to kindergarten. When I was sixteen, I got my driver's license. After turning eighteen, I was considered an adult.

The Origins of Our Calendar

So what about Jesus's birthday? Do we know when he was born?

To answer this question, we have to begin with a quick look at the history of our calendar.[1] Our 365-day calendar—with a 366-day leap year every four years—is based on the amount of time it takes for the earth to complete a full orbit around the sun. This is called a solar year.[2] The advantage of this calendar is that it accurately keeps track of the seasons of the year. This is really important for people like farmers who do important things like grow food.

A version of this solar calendar was established by Julius Caesar around AUC 709 (= 45 BC). The Julian calendar was based on the years from the founding of Rome. AUC is the abbreviation of the Latin phrase *Ab urbe condita*, which means "from the founding of the city." Fun facts: the month of July was named after Julius, and August was named after his son, Augustus.

Alternatively, the 354-day lunar calendar has twelve months based on the phases of the moon. Each month lasts about 29.5 days.[3] One advantage of this calendar is that the moon is a very visible timepiece. There is a clear difference between the black sky of a new moon and the bright sky of the full moon. In modern times, the Islamic calendar is an example of a lunar calendar. However, the problem with this calendar is that it does not keep track of seasons as accurately. So compared with our modern calendar, the lunar calendar loses about 11 days per year.

---

1. For more on the calendar, see Richards, *Mapping Time*, and Steel, *Making Time*. For a more specific look at how the calendar debate impacts the dating of Christmas, see Roll, *Toward the Origins of Christmas*, 57–106.

2. The true solar year is 365.2422 days.

3. More precisely, the lunar calendar is 354.367 days. Each lunar cycle is 29 days, 12 hours, 44 minutes, and 3 seconds.

A variation of the lunar calendar is called the lunisolar calendar. This calendar bases the twelve months of the year on the lunar cycle, but it adds an extra month every few years to keep the calendar aligned with the seasons created by the solar year. Examples of this type of calendar include the Hebrew, Buddhist, Chinese, Japanese, and Korean calendars. In addition, for most Christians, the date of Easter is computed using this calendar system, which is why Easter falls on a different date each year.

Our division between BC and AD is based on a dating system introduced in AD 525 by a monk named Dionysius "the Humble" whose aim was to determine the date of the church's annual Easter celebrations. His dating system began with the first year of Jesus's life. Subsequently, this became known as AD 1 (= AUC 754).[4] AD abbreviates the Latin phrase, *anno Domini*, which means "in the year of our Lord."[5] The years prior to the birth of Jesus eventually became known by the Latin phrase *ante Christum natum*, meaning "before the birth of Christ." In English, this became the abbreviation BC, meaning "Before Christ." We should also note that there is no year zero; instead, the BC/AD scheme goes from 1 BC to AD 1.

Unfortunately, the Julian calendar was actually 11 minutes and 14 seconds longer than the solar year, which caused the calendar to drift over time.[6] To fix this problem, Pope Gregory XIII introduced the Gregorian calendar in 1582, which is the basis of our modern calendar.[7] Not all churches accepted this "innovation." So, the Eastern Orthodox Church observes Christmas on January 7 (which is actually December 25 on their calendar). Rejecting a more accurate dating system may be hard for modern people to understand. Isn't newer, better?

---

4. There is a debate about whether Dionysius thought that Jesus was born in 1 BC or AD 1. On Jesus's birth in AD 1, see Declercq ("Dionysius Exiguus," 242–46) who links this to the traditional date of Jesus's conception on March 25. Alternatively, on Jesus's birth in 1 BC, see Steel (*Making Time*, 109–11) who ties this to Jesus's circumcision on January 1 claiming this was the beginning of his first year.

5. The full Latin phrase *anno Domini Nostri Jesu Christi* means "in the year of our Lord Jesus Christ."

6. The Julian year averages 365.25 days, but the solar year is 365.2422 days.

7. The Gregorian year of 365.2425 days is closer to the solar year of 365.2422 days. To correct the Julian calendar's drift, a leap year (366 days) is added every four years, but any year divisible by 100 is not a leap year (e.g., AD 100, 200, 300) unless it is also divisible by 400 (e.g., AD 400, 800, 1200). By the time of this reform, there was a ten-day drift, so when the new calendar was implemented, the date skipped from October 4, 1582, to October 15, 1582. This difference in time also accounts for the difference between some celebrations of Christmas between December 25 and January 7.

While in modern times we are always craving the newest and greatest things, there was a time when "new" things were looked upon with skepticism. Maybe you know someone like this. Do you know someone who always wears their favorite sweater? I can relate to not wanting to change. For the first twenty-five years of my life, I only ate peanut butter sandwiches for lunch. Likewise when the Gregorian calendar was introduced, there were people who preferred the old system.

Nowadays, we still use the Gregorian calendar. However, it has become popular to substitute BCE, meaning "Before the Common Era," for BC, and CE, meaning "Common Era," for AD.[8] While the terms may have changed, the reason for the division still exists. Our modern, western calendar is based upon the birth of Jesus.

Let's think about that for a moment.

There is something significantly powerful about the fact that Christmas still marks our dates and times. Whenever we think about the date, whether it be 1969, 1999, or 2019, we are connecting our days to one of the most significant days in human history—the day that Jesus was born. The coming of Jesus forever changed history.

Look at today's date and remember that it is counting from the year of Jesus's birth. Whatever year it may be, the date is a declaration that it has been so many years, months, and days since Jesus was born. Each year that passes since 1975 tells me how old I am. Each year since AD 1 tells me how long ago Jesus came to the earth.

So, the next time you look at your calendar, try to remember how your own life was changed by the coming of Jesus. Consider how you can live your day because of that change.

Someone Failed Math

Okay, but how accurate is this date?

Let's begin by investigating the dates connected with Jesus's birth in the Gospels. Matthew tells us that Jesus was born during the reign of King Herod the Great (Matthew 2:1–12). However, if you've ever missed a math or history problem, then you're in good company with Dionysius because he did not take into account the date of King Herod's death.[9] It turns out

8. Because this book is about Christmas, it will use the traditional BC and AD notations.

9. Dionysius was actually quite excellent at math and history. He just appears to have

that Herod died somewhere between March 12 and April 11 in 4 BC.[10]
We also are told that Herod killed all the children under two (Matthew
2:16). So to be safe, we can assume a two-year window for Jesus's birth. That
means that Jesus was born somewhere between 6 to 4 BC.

However, we run into problems in Luke 2:1–2. Luke appears to connect Jesus's birth to a census under the governor of Syria, Publius Sul-
picius Quirinius.[11] When Quirinius took his post as governor of Syria,
Judea was annexed because of the removal of Herod's son Archelaus. The
census was performed for tax purposes. This census brings challenges for
determining the actual birth year of Jesus because Quirinius became the
governor of Syria around AD 6. However, King Herod the Great died
about ten years earlier in 4 BC.

Explanations range from saying that either Matthew or Luke got
their dates jumbled or trying to explain how these two dates really do
correspond.[12] One of the simplest ways to harmonize these two dates is to
affirm that Jesus was born during the time of King Herod but before the
time of Quirinius by translating Luke 2:2 as "This census took place *before*
Quirinius was governor of Syria."[13]

Another approach examines how Luke arranges his stories in his Gospel. Luke 1:1–4 opens with a claim to give an "orderly" account of Jesus's
life. However, we should not fall into the trap of thinking that Luke must
mean that he is telling his stories in a clear historical order. Rather, Luke is
guided by thematically ordering the stories of Jesus.

---

chosen a different set of data for calculating the year of Jesus's birth.

10. Josephus, *Antiquities* 17.190–91; *Jewish Wars* 1.665.

11. Tacitus, *Annals* 6.41; Josephus, *Antiquities* 18.1–10; *Jewish War* 7.253.

12. For various explanations and the issues about the census, see Nolland, *Luke*,
1:99–101. Tertullian (*Against Marcion* 4.19.10) thought the census occurred under the
governorship of C. Sentius Saturnius (about 9–3 BC). Some, like William Ramsay (*Bearing of Recent Discovery on the Trustworthiness of the New Testament*, 238–300, 293), have
fabricated an earlier Syrian posting of Quirinius such as a co-governorship. The modern
rejection of the historicity of Luke's understanding of the census began with D. F. Strauss's
The Life of Jesus Critically Examined in 1835.

13. See the NIV translation note to support this translation. The main issue is the
syntax related to the word "first, before" (Greek, *prōtē*). Does it mean "first" and modify
"census" (Greek, *apographē*) to mean "first census"? Or does it mean "before" and relate
to the verb "he became" (Greek, *egeneto*) so that we get "before he became governor"?
Translating this passage as "before Quirinius" has been argued by many including
Lagrange, "Où en est la question du recensement de Quirinius?" 60–84, and Barnett,
"ἀπογραφή and ἀπογράφεσθαι in Luke 2:1–5," 377–80.

For example, Luke 3:20 tells us that John the Baptist was put in prison, but the next verse tells us about Jesus's baptism. From the other Gospels, we know that John baptized Jesus, but according to Luke, John is in jail! If we stuck to a historical order, then we would have to ask Luke, "Who baptized Jesus?" So, what is going on? Luke has intentionally omitted John's name from Luke 3:21 because he wants a clear narrative break between the ministries of John and Jesus. After John's ministry ends, Jesus's ministry begins. Thus, Luke's arrangement of material is guided by his thematic purpose.

Luke's thematic ordering may have motivated linking Quirinius's census with Jesus's birth. Luke mentions this census because it was a sign of Roman imperial power and dominance. By mentioning the census, Luke includes a critique of the Roman government. What kind of government makes a poor, pregnant woman travel 85 miles to be counted for tax purposes? This negative view of leaders counting people is also likely based upon the story of God punishing David for taking a census (2 Samuel 24). In contrast to the rulers who count their people to exploit them, the Messiah is born to free his people from exploitation.[14]

Luke's Gospel is also aware of Matthew's dating of Jesus's birth during the days of Herod (6–4 BC). Luke's awareness is confirmed when we look at two groups of evidence from Luke's Gospel. First, Luke 1:5 tells us that John the Baptist's birth was announced during Herod's reign, and Luke 1:36 connects Mary's pregnancy within six months of this announcement. This six-month window between the announcements of John's birth and Jesus's birth makes it quite plausible that Luke knows that Jesus was born during Herod's reign.[15]

Second, we can make a series of calculations backward from the time of Jesus's ministry. According to Luke 3:1–3, John began to baptize people during the fifteenth year of Emperor Tiberius's reign. We can date this fifteenth year somewhere between August 19, AD 28, and December 31, AD 29. So, we can assume that Jesus began his ministry shortly after this time, which would be around AD 29 or 30.[16] This estimate is important

---

14. Horsley, *Liberation of Christmas*, 33–38. Just as David's census led to the "greater good" of building the Jewish temple, so the Roman census led to the "greater good" of the birth of Jesus.

15. Brown, *Birth of the Messiah*, 547–48.

16. Some people use the Gospel of John to date Jesus's ministry beginning in AD 27–28 based upon the claim that it took forty-six years to build the temple (John 2:20) and Josephus (*Antiquities* 15.11.1) dating the beginning of the temple's construction to 20–19 BC. This datapoint is more difficult because it occurs during John's version of

because Luke 3:23 reports that Jesus "was *about* thirty years old when he began his ministry."

Luke uses the word "about" (Greek, *hōsei*) to indicate that he has rounded this number. A rounded number means that Jesus could be a few years older or younger than thirty when he was baptized by John and began his ministry. Luke highlights the age of thirty because it was considered to be an age of maturity (Numbers 4:3).[17] Using our math skills, we can calculate the difference between AD 29–30 and 6–4 BC (remembering there is no year-zero). Thus, we can determine that Jesus was thirty-two to thirty-five years old when he began his public ministry. However, if we used the date of Quirinus's census in AD 6, then Jesus would only be twenty-three or twenty-four years old. Thus, it appears that Luke also dates Jesus's birth near the end of Herod's reign, not Quirinius's census.

Since we're having so much fun with numbers, let's look at the duration of Jesus's ministry and the year of his crucifixion. We get these data from John's Gospel. We assume that Jesus's ministry was at least three years long because John mentions Jesus attending three Passover festivals during his ministry (John 2:13; 6:4; 11:15). Further, John describes Jesus being crucified by Pontius Pilate (who reigned in AD 26–37) on a Friday before Passover (John 19:14, 16). According to the Jewish calendar, this date was Nissan 14. This gives us two choices to date his death—Jesus either died April 7, AD 30, or April 3, AD 33. Since we've seen that Jesus began his ministry around AD 29–30, then Jesus would have been crucified on April 3, AD 33.[18]

Jesus's temple act (John 2:13–25). John places this event at the beginning of Jesus's ministry, while Matthew 21:12–17, Mark 11:15–19, and Luke 19:45–48 portray it at the end. We don't know if John adjusted the date when he moved the story.

17. Leviticus 27:2–7 divides a person's life as one month to five years, five years to twenty-five, twenty-five to sixty, and over sixty. While later than our New Testament times, the life stages of a Jewish male were described in the third century AD as: "At five years of age [one is ready] for Scripture; at ten, for Mishnah; at thirteen for [keeping] the commandments; at fifteen for Talmud; at eighteen for marriage; at twenty for pursuing [a trade]" (*Mishnah 'Abot* 5.21).

18. For more discussions on these dates, see Meier, *Marginal Jew*, 372–409; Donfried, "Chronology, New Testament," 1:1011–22; Hoehner and Brown, "Chronology," 134–38. If we use Matthew, Mark, and Luke's chronology, which has Jesus die on Passover (Nissan 15, Matthew 26:18–19; Mark 14:12; Luke 22:11), then the date would be either AD 27 or AD 34. Some people resolve the different accounts by arguing that Matthew, Mark, and Luke follow an Essene solar calendar, while John uses the official lunisolar calendar.

Thus, the evidence from both Matthew and Luke points to shifting Jesus's birth to 6–4 BC, while his ministry began around AD 29–30. According to John, he died on April 3, AD 33. Even with these small correctives, the principle still stands that every moment of our life is counted based on the birth of Jesus. The next time you check your smartphone or ask what the date is, remember you know that time because of the birth of Jesus.

What Day *Was* Christmas?

Okay, we know Jesus was born around 6–4 BC, but was he really born on December 25?[19]

While my birthday falls on the same date every calendar year, I have friends born in other countries, like Korea, whose birthdays are based on a different calendar system. Because they do not use the western Gregorian calendar, their birthday "changes" each year when looked through my western eyes. However, from their perspective, they have a fixed date, and it is my calendar that changes.

It turns out that one's culture actually determines even something as "fixed" as a calendar day. Having different calendars isn't new. Even during Jesus's day, some Jewish people used a solar calendar, while others used a lunisolar calendar.[20]

When it comes to Jesus's birthday, we often approach Christmas with the idea that a birthday corresponds to the exact point in time when that person was born. So, it's easy for people to assume that Christmas was really Jesus's birthday.

December 25 occurs during the Northern Hemisphere's winter when it snows in many places in the United States and Europe. It's no wonder many of us imagine a white Christmas. Anything sunny or without snow, almost

19. For those wishing to dive deeper into the discussion, the best place to start is Roll's *Toward the Origins of Christmas*. Alternatively, another good work is Talley, *Origins of the Liturgical Year*. See also, Kelly, *Origins of Christmas*. Shorter treatments include Crump, "Christmas Day," n.p. and Roll, "Christmas and Its Cycle," 3:551–57. Roll updates and supplements Smith, "Christmas and Its Cycle," 3:655–60.

20. Because the Bible does not present any complete calendar system, various Jewish groups disputed how to keep track of time. A 364-day solar calendar is described in Jubilees 6:30, 32; 1 Enoch 72–82; and the Temple Scroll of the Dead Sea Scrolls. In the Mishnah (*Megilla* 1:4; *Nedarim* 8:5), a lunisolar calendar is described where an extra month is added every two to three years. Among the Qumran literature, the *Commentary on Habakkuk* indicates this group observed the Day of Atonement on a different day than their opponents.

seems un-Christmas-like to us. (Sorry, Florida and Hawaii!) Even though, if Jesus was really born in December, there wouldn't have been snow because it only rarely snows in southern Israel during the winter. So, I hate to break it to us, but there probably was no first "White Christmas."

In fact, Christmas didn't exactly start as a birthday party for Jesus. "Christmas" is an abbreviated form of "Christ's mass," which was the name of the church services on this day. It comes from the Old English expression, *Cristes Maesses*, which was first used in AD 1038. Our first recorded Christmas service on December 25 was in AD 336, which is over three hundred years after Jesus's birth![21]

For some of us growing up in the church, we might have been shocked when one of our friends did a quick internet search and told us that Wikipedia says that Jesus wasn't born on December 25. For others of us, we might be surprised that anyone actually accepted this as the "real" birthday of Jesus. Thinking that this is some trenchant part of a war on Christmas, we might go talk to our pastor, read our Bibles, or go explore what "Christian" authors or apologists have to say. Then we discover it's true that we don't actually know the precise date when Jesus was born.

This is because the Gospel writers weren't concerned with precise days and times for most events in Jesus's life and ministry. We don't know the day of Jesus's baptism. We don't know when Jesus taught the Lord's Prayer. We don't know when Jesus fed five thousand people. We don't know when Jesus calmed the storm on the Sea of Galilee. The one notable exception is that the Gospel writers gave us the days of Jesus's last week of life culminating in his death and resurrection.[22]

We need to abandon our notions of ancient people who act like us by pulling out smartphones and recording with precision every moment of every event. They didn't have their digital assistants that could remind them of when things should occur. But this doesn't mean that they didn't care about events. They just approached events with a different set of values and saw

21. *Cristes Maesses* is first found in *The Anglo-Saxon Chronicle* in AD 1038. There are traditionally three masses celebrated—at midnight (Angel's Mass), at dawn (Shepherd's Mass), and during the day (Mass of the Divine Word). The earliest authentic document dating a Christmas as December 25 is Furius Dionysius Philocalus's *Chronograph*, written in AD 354, but the source reference can be dated to AD 336 (Roll, *Towards the Origins of Christmas*, 83–86).

22. However, we run into a different set of problems when dating Jesus's crucifixion because Matthew, Mark, and Luke seem to identify it occurring on the Passover (Nissan 15). In contrast, John identifies it occurring the day before Passover (Nissan 14).

time differently. Try spending a day without looking at the clock or a calendar. The Gospel writers were more concerned with the *significance* of Jesus's birth than with telling us precisely when it happened.

Why December 25?

While the majority of the world celebrates Christmas on December 25, some Christians today celebrate on January 6 or 7.[23] Although the Bible gives us some clues about the year of Jesus's birth, the Bible never offers us any solid clues about the time of year.

Digging deeper, we discover that during the first three centuries of the church's existence, there were a variety of opinions about the date of Christmas.[24] One of the earliest witnesses, Clement of Alexandria (AD 150–215) favored November 18, while another work, *On Computing the Paschal Feast* 18–23 (AD 243), argued for March 28. In fact, during this time Christians celebrated Jesus's birth on a whole variety of "not-December 25" days including January 6 or 10, March 25 or 28, April 18 or 19, May 20, or November 18.

Our earliest witness to a December 25 date comes from Julius Africanus (AD 221) whose main concern was dating the angel's announcement to Mary about Jesus's birth on March 25 (Luke 1:26–38).[25] By adding nine months, we arrive on December 25 for Jesus's birth. However, we also have some writers, like Origen (AD 185–254) who condemned the celebration of Jesus's birthday as something too "secular" for Christians.[26] That's right, some Christians wanted to cancel Christmas.

So when did Christians start consistently celebrating Christmas on December 25?

During the fourth and fifth centuries.

But why? What happened?

23. Christmas is celebrated on December 25 by the Protestant, Anglican, Episcopal, and Roman Catholic churches, while it is celebrated on January 6 by the Armenian church and January 7 by some Eastern Orthodox.

24. See appendix for date lists. Roll, *Towards the Origins of Christmas*, 77–87, 100–105, 117.

25. Africanus records the annunciation on the first day of the year, which would be March 25. He writes, " . . . the number of 5,500 years as the period up to the advent of the Word of salvation, that was announced to the world in the time of the sway of the Cæsars" (Africanus, *Chronology* 1).

26. Origen, *Leviticus, Homily 8*.

A popular theory is that when Emperor Constantine made Christianity a "legal" religion of the Roman Empire in AD 313, he replaced the Roman festivals with Christian celebrations including Christmas. A guy named Philocalus records in his *Chronograph* that Christians in the West (Rome) celebrated Christmas as early as AD 336. Others will cite a tradition that credits Pope Julius I with establishing the date around AD 350.[27] So, yes, Christians in Rome were celebrating Christmas on December 25 during the time of Constantine.

But here's the problem. Constantine didn't live in Rome at this time. He lived in another city, Constantinople, which was located in the eastern part of the Roman Empire.[28] And it turns out that Christians in the East weren't pushing to celebrate Christmas on December 25 until about fifty years after Constantine died! Thus, Gregory of Nazianzen preached a sermon in Constantinople in AD 381 claiming to be the originator of Christmas in that city. John Chrysostom claims to bring the celebration of Christmas on December 25 to another eastern city, Antioch, in AD 386–388.[29]

So, if Constantine didn't start the Roman celebration of Christmas on December 25, then why did it happen? To get at this question, we have to understand a little bit about the church during this time. Before Constantine, Christianity had been an illegal, persecuted religion. After Constantine, Christians were free to practice their beliefs openly.

When churches were finally able to come out of hiding, this allowed, for the first time, church leaders to be able to really start talking with each other. When they began to talk, they found out (surprise!) that they didn't always agree with each other.

Because of this freedom, the church was able to gather together in order to discuss, formulate, and crystalize key ideas. So, they began to sort out important doctrines about the three-in-one nature of God called the "Trinity" at councils like Nicaea in AD 325.[30] They tackled the thorny issue

27. This tradition is cited by John of Nikiû (about AD 900).

28. Constantine moved the capital to Byzantium in AD 324 and renamed it Constantinople in AD 330.

29. Talley, "Constantine," 192–96; Roll, *Towards the Origins of Christmas*, 117. Chrysostom's sermon indicates that celebrating Christmas on December 25 began in the West, possibly Rome. However, in the East, Christmas was celebrated on January 6 until the fourth century. In Palestine, it was celebrated on January 6 until the seventh century (Egeria, *Itinerarium* 25). The Armenian church has never accepted December 25.

30. The Nicene Creed doesn't use the word "Trinity," but it mentions the Father, Son, and Holy Spirit, which helped lay the groundwork for Trinitarian discussions. For more

of Jesus being fully God and fully human at the Council of Chalcedon in AD 451.[31] They also were in the process of confirming the sixty-six books of the Bible with Athanasius's Easter Letter in AD 367. In this kind of climate, it shouldn't surprise us that the church was also sorting out which days to celebrate its major festivals, including Christmas.

Some Christians calculated the date of Christmas on December 25 in relation to other significant biblical events.[32] For example, Jesus's birth was calculated as nine months after Jesus's conception on March 25. March 25 was considered a special date for various reasons. For some, it was connected to the creation of the sun. Alternatively, some believed that Jesus was conceived on the same day that he died.[33] Others thought that he was conceived on this date because it was the spring equinox (the first day of spring).[34] Still others used John the Baptist's conception during the fall equinox (the first day of fall) on September 25 to calculate Jesus's conception on March 25 and his birth on December 25.[35]

For other Christians, December 25 may have been chosen as an alternative to three other popular Roman religious festivals[36] occurring during the winter solstice (the longest night of the year).[37] One festival

---

on the Trinity, see chapter 11.

31. One of the most significant controversies was with the Arians, who emphasized the humanity of Jesus. The other major controversy was with Nestorius, who was accused of teaching that Jesus's distinct divine and human natures were not fully joined int he person of Jesus (Roll, *Towards the Origins of Christmas*, 177–78).

32. This is called the "Calculation Hypothesis." Recent support is found in Talley, *Origins of the Liturgical Year*, 91–99. The catalyst for the modern discussion is Duchesne, *Origines du cultechrétien*. For a review, see Roll, *Towards the Origins of Christmas*, 87–96.

33. *Rosh Hashana* (second century) has Jewish patriarchs' birthdays and death-days coincide. Alternatively, Epiphanius *Commentary on Luke*, folio 74 (fifth century) connects Jesus's conception and passion to April 6 and his birth to January 6. Talley, *Origins of the Liturgical Year*, 81–83.

34. In the northern hemisphere, the dates of the spring and fall equinoxes have shifted to March 19–21 and September 21–23.

35. Jesus is conceived six months after John according to Luke 1:36. The oldest record of this type of computation is *De solstitiis et aequinoctiis* (second half of the fourth century). Both John Chrysostom and Augustine make similar arguments. Talley, *Origins of the Liturgical Year*, 94–95; Roll, *Towards the Origins of Christmas*, 97–98.

36. This is called the "History of Religions Hypothesis," which may go back to Dionysius Bar-Salibi (twelfth century). Hermann Usener (1889) and Bernard Botte (1932) shaped the modern conversation. More recently, see Roll, *Toward the Origins of Christmas* (1995). For a clear overview of these festivals, see Kelly, *Origins of Christmas*, 78–83.

37. While December 25 was the ancient date for the winter solstice, the modern date

celebrated on December 17–23, called *Saturnalia*, honored Saturn, the Roman god of prosperity. A second festival, established by Emperor Aurelian in AD 274, occurred on December 25 in order to celebrate a newly minted supreme sun god, *Deus Sol Invictus* ("Divine Unconquered Sun").[38] Thirdly, Roman soldiers celebrated the birth of the Persian sun god, Mithras, on December 25.[39]

However, it is unlikely that Christians were attempting to co-opt secular cultural customs to legitimize Christianity since early Christians consistently identified themselves in opposition to their culture and other religions.[40] More likely, Christians in Rome began to hold Christmas celebrations on December 25 as an alternative to what they considered pagan holiday celebrations. (Others speculate that Aurelian began the *Sol Invictus* festival to counter Christian practices.)[41]

What do we make of all of this? First, it's clear that many Christians were celebrating Christmas prior to the fourth century. This means that the Christmas celebration was not started as a Roman holiday. However, there was no consistent date for this celebration. Second, it appears that beginning in the fourth century, Christians moved toward being unified in celebrating Jesus's birth on December 25, just as they were becoming unified about their beliefs about God and the Bible. Third, Christmas became a clear and tangible way for Christians to publicly celebrate the incarnation of Jesus—the idea that God became a human to dwell among and redeem humankind (John 1:1–18; Philippians 2:5–11; Colossians 1:15–20; Hebrews 1:1–4)—and this was done in contrast to Roman festivals.

---

falls between December 20 and 23, with the 21st and 22nd as the most common.

38. The Roman cult of the sun was established in AD 218 by Elagabalus but was initially rejected by the Romans. However, under Emperor Aurelian in AD 274 a festival was established called the "Birth of the Unconquered Sun" (*Natalis Solis Invicti*). There was a chariot race on December 25 as documented by the *Chronograph* (AD 354). Later, Julian the Apostate (*Hymn to King Helios*) attempted to reinstate Roman religions including this festival in AD 362.

39. According to the myth, Mithras killed the cosmic bull from which the world was made. He was taken into heaven in a fiery chariot. He shared his birthday with the sun god.

40. For example, Pope Leo I (*Patrologia Latina* 54.218, died AD 461) criticized Christians who bowed to the rising sun. Origen (*Leviticus, Homily 8*; AD 185–254) objected to any celebration of Christmas because of imitating pagan celebration of birthdays.

41. If we privilege Aurelian's (AD 274) *Sol Invictus* festival, then Christian Christmas was second. If we see Africanus (AD 221) as representing an established Christmas festival on December 25, then *Sol Invictus* is second. Kelly, *Origins of Christmas*, 78–80.

So, we want to avoid the mistake that some people make by claiming that the origin of Christmas is a secular holiday. However, we also want to avoid the other mistake of saying that December 25 was the actual, historical day of Jesus's birth.

Christians today are known for offering "alternatives" to the broader culture like proms, Halloween festivals, or music. Likewise, Christians in the ancient world seemed to have had the same mindset with Christmas. Rather than worshiping the birthdays of the false sun gods, Christians chose to celebrate the birth of the true Son of God. During this time, Christians drew upon texts like Malachi 4:2, which says, "The sun of righteousness will rise with healing in its wings," and John 8:12, in which Jesus declares, "I am the light of the world." Thus, some Christians linked Jesus as the "Son" of God with the "sun."

Just as Jesus can be described with images of sun and light, so Jesus tells his followers, "You are the light of the world. A city built on a hill cannot be hid. No one after lighting a lamp puts it under the bushel basket" (Matthew 5:14–15). Light imagery is connected with ideas of truth and proper guidance. So, Christmas can be a time for Christians to share Jesus's light with the world.

We can share this light, not simply by recounting the Christmas story, but also through how we treat others. We see this light whenever we see people ringing their bells to elicit donations for the unfortunate. We feel this light's warmth wherever churches or organizations provide hot meals and safe places to sleep. Illumination comes whenever toys are donated to children who might not receive presents. We see a brightness when carolers sing Christmas songs in retirement homes. But we also see this light in how we treat each other during the holiday season. How can we be this light by showing others extra kindness, patience, and love during this season?

Sacred *and* Secular

Some complain that the origins of Christmas are just another example of the evils of religious syncretism. They go on further to dismantle Christmas traditions, including the giving and receiving of gifts, the stories of Santa Claus, Advent wreaths, Yuletide greetings, and Christmas trees.[42]

42. Nissenbaum, *Battle for Christmas*, 178–88, 195–97. He argues that the American tradition was introduced to combat the selfishness and consumerism of children.

When it comes to Christmas, it can be tempting to go to one of two extremes. Do we merely imitate our culture and its values when it comes to our Christmas celebrations? Is our church known for the biggest and best Christmas programs? Do we give away the greatest number of presents? Do we have the largest Christmas tree? The most joyous angelic choir? The most realistic animals? Or do we wage war against cultural Christmas and reject anything that does not smack of biblical "purity"? Do we reject anything that is new? Do we get rid of Santa, presents, hot cocoa, and Christmas trees?

Rejecting Christmas is not just a modern phenomenon. The first recorded rejection of Christmas comes from Origen (AD 185–254). More recently, the Puritans waged war against Christmas as being too pagan and unbiblical. They outlawed Christmas in Scotland in 1561 (it was not a legal holiday until 1958) and declared it as a day of penance in England in 1647. In the United States, the Massachusetts Bay Colony outlawed Christmas from 1659 to 1681. In fact, Christmas wasn't a legal holiday in the United States until 1836 when Alabama became the first state to make it an official holiday. More popular traditions like the first National Christmas Tree Lighting did not occur until 1913.

We certainly need to be wary of ways that our Christmas celebrations in the church have taken our eyes off Jesus. We can ask ourselves simple questions like, "Do we get more excited about opening our presents at home or going to church to celebrate Jesus's birth?" If you're like me, it's easy to get caught up in the excitement and spectacle of the holiday.

More challenging is to find a place where we Christians neither reject cultural traditions nor blindly follow them. Is it possible to occupy a position where Christians look to embody and redeem Christmas? What would it look like for Christians to avoid simply adopting traditions based on our culture, but rather transform and redeem these traditions?

At the heart of the story of Christmas is the story of the incarnation. Christians believe that the Son of God was born as the human Jesus. In other words, God became a first-century Jew, taking on Jewish customs, Jewish language, Jewish culture, and so forth in order to redeem the world. Likewise, are there ways for Christians to embody Christmas in order to redeem it? In what ways can we adapt our Christmas celebrations in light of our modern customs, languages, and culture in order to bring God's presence to our world and our time?

Christmas becomes a lesson for us all year long. Every day we as Christians are faced with choices of whether we will follow cultural trends or whether we will live distinct lives. The food we eat and drink, the clothes we wear, the homes where we live, the transportation we use—all of these are products of our culture. We build bridges with others through our common experiences. But we also need to ask ourselves how we can point to something miraculous beyond our everyday experiences. Jesus came to the earth as an ordinary baby, but his mundane existence pointed to the miraculous.

So how can we point to the miraculous in our everyday experiences? Certainly, as a starting point, we can thank God for our food, clothes, homes, and transportation (and many of us do in our prayers). But can we do more? Are we making responsible food and clothing purchases from fair trade companies that seek to promote justice and human dignity? Do we donate food and clothing to those in need? What if our homes were known as places of hospitality and kindness for our neighbors and friends? Can we use our vehicles to transport friends, classmates, children, or the elderly to places where they need to go? Are we supportive within our community of services that provide shelter and transportation to people in need? Do our churches stand up for racial justice because everyone is created in the image of God?

Just as early Christians sought to redeem their cultural celebrations to a sun god, can we look for ways to redeem our cultural celebrations to our consumeristic god?[43] With a mindset of redemption, we don't need to be fearful of how our culture celebrates Christmas. But we do need to be attentive.

The good news is that many thoughtful Christians have already led the way for us. Churches like the Salvation Army collect donations during the Christmas season. Christian homeless shelters provide warm beds and hot meals. Organizations like Operation Christmas Child help mobilize giving gifts to children. Of course, there's always more to be done. Maybe you've got your own dreams that could be made a reality this season. Maybe this Christmas will be your chance to join with others helping those in need. Maybe you're already helping, and your Christmas surprise is the new group of extra volunteers working by your side.

43. Horsley and Tracy, *Christmas Unwrapped.* On the commercialization of Christmas in the United States, see Schmidt, *Consumer Rites,* 105–91; Barnett, *American Christmas,* 79–101. In 1906 one writer bemoaned, "We are really slaves of our Christmas shopping lists" (Barnett, *American Christmas,* 183).

So, this Christmas, rather than rejecting all the trappings of Christmas, let's follow the model of Christ's incarnation to embody and transform them.

Reflection Questions

1. How do you celebrate your birthday? Do you have any birthday traditions? Do you have a favorite birthday cake, pie, or special treat? What does it mean that Christmas is celebrating Jesus's birthday?

2. Did you have any interesting insights about the origins of our modern, western calendar? Have you ever thought about calendars reflecting our cultural differences like the difference between a Korean and American calendar system?

3. Just as our calendar was changed to BC/AD by the coming of Jesus, how has your life been changed by the coming of Jesus?

4. Luke links Jesus's birth to the Roman census in order to critique his government's exploitation of the poor. How do we see the poor being marginalized in our world? What can we do to help the poor?

5. Do you think it is important to celebrate Christmas on December 25? Can you imagine celebrating Christmas in March, April, May, November, or January?

6. Christians were celebrating Christmas before the fourth century, but they began to celebrate Christmas on December 25 as an alternative to pagan celebrations during the winter solstice. To what extent can Christians adopt traditions based on our culture? Are there Christmas traditions that we shouldn't adopt? To what extent do Christians need to be counter-cultural in our Christmas celebrations?

7. Jesus is connected to being the light of the world. Many candlelight church services emphasize this idea. How can Christmas be a time of sharing Jesus's light with the world? Are there areas in your life where you need illumination?

8. How can Christmas inspire us to show others extra kindness, patience, and love during the holiday season and all year round?

Activity: Time with God

This chapter has focused on the origin of our calendars and the decision to celebrate Christmas on December 25. Whenever you see the date, use it to remember Jesus's birth. Can this be a reminder that your day is a gift from God? Ask God to be present with you in the day. When your day is lit by the "sun," can you think of the "Son" of God and ask him to illuminate your path? Consider the rhythms of your life. What do you organize your life around? Is it sports seasons, kids' activities, school, work, vacation, family, and so forth? How important are Sundays? When do you pray? Where do you serve others? Do you read Scripture? Do you journal? Sing worship songs? Would an app or calendar help you create new rhythms that remind you to center your life on Jesus? When you prepare for Christmas this year, consider using an Advent calendar or Advent wreath to mark off each day or week leading up to Christmas.

3

Ruining the Christmas Story— Rediscovering the Call to Keep Telling the Story

G rowing up, my parents taught me the importance of a good story. Good storytellers know how to take a good story and make it better. Some storytellers do this by adding additional facts, insights, and perspectives to the story. A good storyteller can transport you inside the world of the story. A great storyteller makes you forget that he or she is telling the story.

My grandparents grew up in an age before TV or the internet, and they spent their evenings crafting stories and spinning yarns. My grandpa could make painting the side of a barn sound interesting. Other family members are also great storytellers, but they make their stories great by just making stuff up. You're guaranteed to be entertained by their version of an event, even if you're unsure what actually happened.

The Sources of the Christmas Story

When it comes to the Christmas story, we discover that expanding and making additions is nothing new. In our New Testament, the stories of Jesus are found in the first four books called the Gospels—Matthew, Mark, Luke, and John.

To better understand these stories, it can help us to notice that the New Testament is arranged in a rough chronological order. It begins by recounting Jesus's ministry in the Gospels. Then it moves onto the life and growth of the church documented in Acts and the New Testament letters. Finally, it concludes with the end of this world and the beginning of the new world in Revelation.

However, the New Testament books are not arranged according to what was composed first to what was written last. Matthew is not the first book written, and Revelation is not the last book. The first book written was either the tiny letter of Jude (as early as AD 40) or the letter of James (as early as AD 47). It is also possible that the letters of Paul were written first (AD 50–64).[1]

Our Gospels were written much later, probably at least forty years after the death of Jesus (AD 33). Of these Gospels, it turns out that most scholars think that Mark was the first Gospel written (AD 65–75). Then Matthew and Luke were written (AD 80–90).[2] Finally, John was written (AD 90–100).[3] This actually makes sense when you look at each book's length and content. Three of these Gospels—Matthew, Mark, and Luke— tell very similar stories, which get progressively longer. Mark is the shortest book (16 chapters) while Luke (24 chapters) and Matthew (28 chapters) are

---

1. There is considerable debate concerning the dating of New Testament writings. Jude can be dated as early as AD 40 but as late as AD 80. The letter from James's date is dependent upon whether we consider it written before or after Paul's letter to the Galatians (AD 51). It is debated whether 1 Thessalonians or Galatians is Paul's first letter. Paul wrote all his letters between AD 50 and his death in AD 64 or AD 67. For greater details, see Martin and Toney, *New Testament Foundations*.

2. The relationship and order of Matthew, Mark, and Luke is called the "Synoptic Problem." While church tradition favored Matthew's priority (such as Irenaeus, Eusebius, and Augustine), Henry Owen made the first modern argument for Matthean priority in 1764; it was popularized in 1789 by Johann Griesbach. In 1835 Karl Lachmann presented the first modern arguments for the priority of Mark, which have been accepted by a majority of NT scholars today.

3. For a survey of the New Testament, including dates, see Martin and Toney, *New Testament Foundations*.

much longer.[4] The Gospel of John tells an entirely different version of Jesus's story, and we think that his Gospel was written last.

How Mark Almost Ruined Christmas

What's curious is that when we read these four Gospels, only two of them—Matthew and Luke—tell us stories about Jesus's birth. What's even crazier is that if Mark had been the only Gospel written, there might never have been a Christmas!

It turns out that Mark completely skips over the birth of Jesus. He doesn't think it is very important. Instead, he begins with the life and ministry of Jesus in his thirties (Mark 1:9).[5] Since Mark doesn't bother to tell us about the birth of the "greatest gift of all," I like to pretend that he must have been the Grinch who stole Christmas.

So who saved Christmas?

Well, it turns out that two of our Gospel writers—Matthew and Luke—read Mark and thought, "That's weird, no Christmas," and they decided to write Gospels that told the Christmas story.

What's fascinating is that when Matthew and Luke decide to tell the Christmas story, they tell two very different Christmas stories.[6] The most famous difference is that Matthew tells us the story of the magi visiting Jesus, while Luke records the shepherds' visit. We also discover that Matthew's story mainly focuses upon the experiences of Joseph, while Luke focuses upon the perspective of Mary.[7]

While our churches tend to weave together the stories of Matthew and Luke during our Christmas celebrations, let's take a moment to appreciate the unique voices of these two storytellers.

---

4. Alternatively, these three Gospels may have been written from Mark (16 chapters) to Matthew (28 chapters) to Luke-Acts (52 chapters).

5. See Luke 3:23 and the previous chapter for calculating Jesus's age.

6. One of the most complete studies comparing the birth stories is Brown, *Birth of the Messiah*.

7. Horsley (*Liberation of Christmas*, 90) argues that Luke presents Mary as "specifically commissioned as the principal agent of deliverance in the infancy narratives."

Matthew Makes His Mark

Matthew begins by telling us about Jesus's heritage giving us the genealogy of Jesus (Matthew 1:1–17). He starts with Abraham and traces the genealogy through the royal lineage of David. By beginning with Jesus's ancestors, Matthew ties the story of Jesus into the story of Israel. As he tells the stories of Jesus's birth, Matthew weaves Jesus's story into the larger story of Israel by demonstrating how the events of Jesus's life fulfill Old Testament prophecies.

The birth story is told with breathtaking speed through Joseph's eyes (Matthew 1:18–25). First, Joseph discovers that Mary is pregnant. Then, he decides "to divorce her quietly" (v. 19 NIV). Then, an angel appears in order to tell him that Mary is still a virgin and that the baby is from the Holy Spirit. Then, the baby is born, and Joseph names him "Jesus."

The scene then switches away from Joseph to the story of the magi (Matthew 2:1–12). They follow a star that leads them to King Herod whom they foolishly ask, "Where is the [other] king of the Jews?" Herod schemes to rid himself of Jesus by enlisting the Jewish religious leaders to help the magi find the child. He then sends the magi to Bethlehem with the expectation that they will report the child's location. When the magi find Mary and Jesus, they give him their precious gifts. Finally, the magi return to their own country after they are warned in a dream not to return to Herod.

Matthew closes the story with Joseph's family fleeing to Egypt (Matthew 2:13–15). Then, Herod kills all the children under two in Bethlehem (Matthew 2:16–18). Finally, Joseph's family returns to Nazareth after Herod's death (Matthew 2:19–23).

Looking at Luke

Luke takes an entirely different approach. He weaves the stories of the birth of John the Baptist with the birth of Jesus. So, Luke begins with an angel revealing to the elderly priest Zechariah that he and his wife Elizabeth would have a son named John (Luke 1:5–25). This revelation occurs while Zechariah was serving in the temple. Because he didn't believe the angel, Zechariah is struck mute. The story highlights God listening and faithfully responding to this couple's prayers. Through this miracle, God will also undo their shame of being childless.

Within this context of God doing miraculous things, Luke tells us about how Mary learned the surprising news that she is pregnant from the angel Gabriel (Luke 1:26–38). Mary is told that she will name her child "Jesus" and that he will be the Son of God who would rule on David's throne. The story begins with the angel calling Mary a "favored one," and ends with Mary's humble response that she is the Lord's "servant." To verify this news, Mary is told that Elizabeth is pregnant. When Mary visits Elizabeth, she offers a song of praise about God's faithfulness to his people (Luke 1:39–56).

Luke 1:57–80 describes the birth of John the Baptist. After the child is born, both Elizabeth and Zechariah name him John, which results in Zechariah being able to speak again. Zechariah's first words are a prophecy about John's future ministry as someone who would prepare the way for the Messiah, Jesus.

Finally, the story of Jesus's birth is told in Luke 2:1–20. While Matthew simply puts Mary and Joseph in Bethlehem, Luke gives the backstory of a census that requires them to travel to that village. Luke also gives other details like Jesus being wrapped in swaddling clothes and being placed in a manger. We also learn about angels appearing to shepherds to proclaim the birth of Jesus. And, of course, the shepherds visit the child.

After the child is born, he is circumcised and named "Jesus" (Luke 2:21). Then, Luke concludes the stories about the baby Jesus when he is taken to the temple (Luke 2:22–38). At the temple, the family encounters two elderly folk, Simeon and Anna, who have been waiting to see the Messiah. Finally, they return home to Nazareth (Luke 2:39–40). However, there is no mention of the troubles caused by King Herod or their flight to Egypt.

But Luke isn't done telling the stories of Jesus. He tells us the only story we have about Jesus's childhood (Luke 2:41–52). This story will remind the readers, one more time, about who Jesus's real Father is. When Jesus was twelve, he travels with his family to Jerusalem for the Passover. When he becomes lost, his parents look for him for three days! They eventually find him among the teachers in the temple. Jesus justifies himself by saying that he needed to spend time in his heavenly Father's house.

Possibly the most surprising feature of Luke's account of Jesus's childhood is the location of Jesus's genealogy in Luke 3:23–38. Rather than including it as part of the birth stories like Matthew 1:1–17, Luke places it with stories of Jesus as an adult. He includes the genealogy (Luke 3:23–38) after the story of Jesus's baptism (Luke 3:1–22) but before Jesus's temptation (Luke 4:1–13). The reason for this choice is to highlight that Jesus is the Son of God.

With the baptism, Luke recounts God declaring Jesus to be his Son (Luke 3:22). Drawing upon this theme, Luke traces Jesus's lineage all the way back to Adam, the "son of God" (Luke 3:38). During Jesus's temptation, the Devil opens with the question, "If you are the Son of God . . . " (Luke 4:3). A thread runs through all these stories that Jesus is the true Son of God. This emphasis upon Jesus as the Son of God ties back to Gabriel's announcement to Mary that Jesus would be called the Son of God (Luke 1:35).

I'm Not Surprised

Now that we've looked at the different stories, we should note that differences shouldn't surprise us. Have you ever noticed how different people can tell different versions of the same story?[8]

Growing up, my sister and I would sometimes spend Saturdays together going to a movie or playing in the park. At dinner, my parents would ask us about our day. I would answer with the single word "fine" because I thought that explained pretty clearly what the essence of the day was like. On the other hand, my sister could recount the moments of the day in a play-by-play fashion.

Looking at the actual birth of Jesus, Matthew writes in a spirit that I appreciate. In one verse, he simply says that Jesus was born, and his father Joseph named him "Jesus" (Matthew 1:25).

On the other hand, the Gospel of Luke gives a report that would make my sister proud. Not only does he tell the story of Jesus's birth, but he also gives the backstory of how Jesus's cousin, John the Baptist, was born (Luke 1–2). Further, he turns the story of Jesus into a musical. Characters burst into songs to express their feelings about the event. So, we hear the songs of Mary (Luke 1:46–55), Zechariah (1:67–79), the angels (2:13–14), and Simeon (2:28–32).[9]

---

8. There have been some great works on how social memory works. An accessible introduction to social memory theory is Le Donne, *Historical Jesus: What Can We Know and How Can We Know It?* See also Allison, *Constructing Jesus: Memory, Imagination, History.*

9. Each of these is given a Latin title: the *Magnificat, Benedictus, Gloria in Excelsis Deo,* and *Nunc dimittis.*

The final Gospel, John, takes a different approach. Rather than beginning with stories of Jesus's earthly origins, John goes all the way back to the beginning of creation (John 1:1–3). He claims that Jesus is the divine Word of God who made the whole world. John's opening makes it very clear to his audience that Jesus is more than a mere human. He is the incarnate Word of God. While characters may struggle with Jesus's identity, the audience does not. It is almost with a sigh of relief when Thomas finally declares at the end of the Gospel what the readers have known the whole time, "My Lord and my God" (John 20:28).

When we combine these stories, we get the Christmas we all love. As we read these Christmas stories, remember the main character is Jesus. We never want to lose our focus on Jesus as a result of other details. But can we also pay attention to how many different people are part of the birth stories? We see both single and married senior adults, a young and poor couple, local shepherds, foreign magi, religious leaders, and political rulers. And when we begin to explore this wider cast of characters, we discover that there's room for everyone at Christmas.

Thank goodness we don't just have Mark.

The Prequel

But these weren't the only writers to add to the Christmas story. Just like people today are hungry to know additional information about Jesus's birth, so people in the ancient world wanted to "know more."

Probably the most famous additions, which have come to influence our recollection of Christmas, come from a work called the Infancy Gospel of James. If you are feeling fancy, you can also call it the Protevangelium of James. You won't find this book in your Bible. It's not part of the New Testament. However, a quick search on the internet would allow you to read this "Gospel" quickly.[10]

There isn't some grand conspiracy theory as to why this book isn't in our New Testament. The main reason is simple. Even though the author of this work claimed to have been Jesus's brother James (Infancy Gospel of James 25:1–4), it was written at least a hundred years after James died.

Early Christians like Clement of Alexandria and Tertullian were aware of this work. They did not accept it alongside the other four Gospels found

10. It can be read at www.earlychristianwritings.com. For a scholarly translation with comments, see Schneemelcher, *New Testament Apocrypha*.

in our Bible. Sometimes people fall into the trap of thinking that something must be true just because it is an old tradition. But in reality, the early church did not accept these stories as valid accounts of Jesus's birth. So, we should also look at them and their teachings with skepticism.

Just as Hollywood today loves to produce a "prequel" story for its heroes, the Infancy Gospel of James is a "prequel" story for Jesus.[11] It begins with the miraculous birth of Jesus's mother, Mary. In fact, the main concern of the Infancy Gospel of James is to expand the traditions surrounding Mary.

The Infancy Gospel of James

From the Infancy Gospel of James, we learn that Mary's parents' names were Joachim and Anna. They were very pious Israelites. However, it turns out Mary's parents couldn't have kids, so they prayed to God for a child (Infancy Gospel of James 1:9–11; 2:9—3:8).

Her parents are cast in the mold of other biblical characters who could not have babies—like Abraham and Sarah (Genesis 11:30, 16:1–2, etc.), Isaac and Rebekah (Genesis 25:21), as well as Jacob and Rachael (Genesis 29:31). Like other great heroes from the Bible, God answers their prayer. Mary was their miracle baby.

More significantly, Mary is portrayed like other miracle-children who are dedicated to God's service (Infancy Gospel of James 4:2). Like Samson (Judges 13) and Samuel (1 Samuel 1), Mary is raised in the temple beginning at the age of three (Infancy Gospel of James 7:1–10). Among her tasks, she sews a veil for the temple (Infancy Gospel of James 10:1–10). However, when she turns twelve, the priests decide that Mary should marry an older widower named Joseph (Infancy Gospel of James 8:3—9:7). While this story makes the priests the matchmakers, historically, their marriage would have been arranged by their parents.

We can't know for certain the ages of Mary and Joseph, but this story does reflect the probable age range of Mary. Due to the high mortality rate of women during childbirth, it was common for girls to be married during

11. For an overview of infancy Gospels not found in our Bibles, see Kelly, *Origins of Christmas*, 48–64. Other works that deal with Jesus's childhood include The Infancy Gospel of Thomas (AD 140–170), which describes Jesus from the age of five to twelve. The Arabic Infancy Gospel (fourth or fifth century) focuses upon what the family did in Egypt. The Gospel of Pseudo-Matthew (about AD 800) also tells stories from the time in Egypt including Jesus pacifying a dragon!

their early teenage years around the age of sexual maturity. However, the story has widened the age gap between Mary and Joseph. If we accept the life cycle described by later rabbis, then Joseph would have been in his late teens to early twenties (*Mishnah 'Abot* 5.21).

Now back to the story. Joseph's job was to take care of Mary and preserve her chastity. Out of concern for explaining Mary's perpetual chastity, the Infancy Gospel of James tells us that Jesus's siblings were actually Joseph's children from a previous marriage (Infancy Gospel of James 9:8). Around the age of sixteen, Mary is left by Joseph so he can go build a house (Infancy Gospel of James 12:9). Like Luke's Gospel, the angel Gabriel visits Mary to tell her about her miraculous pregnancy. She also visits her cousin Elizabeth (Infancy Gospel of James 11:1–9; 12:3–9). When Mary is six months pregnant, Joseph returns to find a bit of a surprise (Infancy Gospel of James 13:1)!

Expanding upon Matthew's version of the story, the Infancy Gospel of James delves into Joseph's struggles of what to do with his pregnant wife. Remember, his main job was to keep her "not-pregnant." The story recounts the angel's assurance that this was a miracle from God (Infancy Gospel of James 14:1–8).

Despite Joseph's attempt to keep things quiet, the high priest soon finds out. The high priest decides to judge them via an ancient lie-detector test. (Don't try this at home.) He makes Joseph and Mary drink the water of the "Lord's wrath." Then they are sent out into the desert to see if they would die. Because they end up "not dying," they are considered innocent (Infancy Gospel of James 15:1—16:8).

Weaving the story into Luke's tradition, the Infancy Gospel of James 17:1–5 recalls Augustus's census as the reason for their journey to Bethlehem. In preparation for this long journey, the Infancy Gospel of James adds to our Christmas story the donkey for Mary to sit upon. (However, I haven't seen any Christmas programs include Joseph's son Samuel, who supposedly led the donkey.)

The journey is interrupted by the coming birth of Jesus, so the family must quickly find a cave for shelter. Joseph also goes searching for a midwife to help deliver the baby (Infancy Gospel of James 18:1–2; 19:1–18).

Afterward, a woman named Salome hears the news of the virgin birth. She does not believe it is true, so she performs a gynecological examination to verify Mary's virginity. This leads to her hand being withered for her unbelief. Then her hand is restored after her repentance (Infancy Gospel of James 19:18—20:12).

Next, we return to a narrative inspired by Matthew. We read about the magi's visit. They are presented as astrologers who have seen a bright star in the sky. The star leads them to the cave where they give their gifts of gold, frankincense, and myrrh (Infancy Gospel of James 21:1–12).

Like Matthew's story, Herod tries to kill all the kids under two. However, the Infancy Gospel of James adds the story of God sparing the lives of John the Baptist and Elizabeth. They flee into the mountains, which swallow them up for safety. In his pursuit of John, Herod finds Zechariah and kills him (Infancy Gospel of James 22:1—24:14).

The Infancy Gospel of James is one of our earliest examples of Christians blending the stories of Matthew and Luke and using their imaginations to fill in the blanks by expanding upon the Christmas story. His retelling helps flesh out the story with details relevant to his audience.

Keep Telling the Story

While the Infancy Gospel of James didn't make it into our Bibles, some of his traditions were preserved by the church. The tricky thing with traditions is that we can get so used to our traditions and how things are done that we can confuse our traditions about Christmas with the actual Christmas story.

But as long as we remember the distinction between tradition and history, we can decide which traditions we want to accept or reject. For example, Protestant Christians will reject the Infancy Gospel of James's teaching about Mary's perpetual virginity. However, the tradition of a midwife helping to deliver the baby may be something that is considered plausible. For those traditions that we accept, we can let them capture our imaginations to help make the story come alive.

Think about how quickly you could read the Christmas story in our Bibles. It's only a few chapters. Then think about how long was the last Christmas program that you sat through. Almost every element in our Christmas plays is a product of our fertile imaginations. What did Joseph and Mary wear? What did they say (or sing) to each other? What did the manger look like? How cold was it outside? How many shepherds came to visit Jesus? When did the magi arrive?

I've been at churches that made a big deal about renting camels for their Christmas story to help bring the story of the wise men to life. I've also seen Mary riding on a donkey to help her on the journey to Bethlehem. I've even bought a Christmas nativity set from Bethlehem that has all these characters. My "stable" is a hollowed-out olive tree trunk made to look like a cave to give the set a more "authentic feel."

Well, none of these things are found in our Bible's Christmas stories.

But each of these things does capture our imaginations and makes the story come alive.

The fact is that we all fill in the blanks of the Christmas story to make the story come alive. By making the story come alive, it becomes relatable. When the story comes alive, we are reminded that this story really happened to *real* people two thousand years ago.

Just as Jesus's birth forever changed the lives of his parents and family in surprising ways, so Jesus's birth can change our lives. If God can do the miraculous back then, we should look for ways that God can do the miraculous today.

So how do we look for the miraculous today? Because Mary, Anna, Simeon, and others had cultivated their relationships with God, they were able to capture glimpses of what he was doing while others were clueless. Maybe we need to work on deepening our relationship with God. Maybe it's time to reconnect with others at church. Maybe it's time to pick up our Bible and start reading. Maybe we need to go help someone in need. Maybe we just need to try talking to God throughout the day. Maybe we need to find a quiet place and spend some time alone in silent reflection.

We can try looking for God in the extraordinary. We can't find things that we aren't looking for. The magi spent their lives looking to the stars for signs of the divine. Because they were looking, they saw the heavenly sign. What if we begin looking for how God is acting in this world instead of just chalking things up to hard work and dumb luck? Let's look in wonder at our world for miracles like Christmas.

We can also try looking for God in everyday circumstances. We don't have to shoot for the stars. The shepherds were doing what they did every night when the angels appeared. Maybe we just have to live our regular, ordinary lives, and God will show up. Maybe we'll encounter God through something we read, from words spoken by another person, or through a song that we hear. Remember that God can challenge, affirm, encourage, or teach us through anything.

Reflection Questions

1. What is one of the best stories you've ever heard or watched? What made it so great?

2. Can you imagine a world without the Christmas story? Why do you think Mark skipped the Christmas story?

3. Why do Matthew and Luke tell different versions of the Christmas story? Were there any parts of these differences that stood out and were meaningful for you?

4. What did you think about the Infancy Gospel of James? What are some of the Christmas traditions that this work adds? Do you agree or disagree with any of those traditions? How do you feel about a non-biblical work informing our traditions?

5. How do our churches fill out and expand the Christmas story with their Christmas celebrations? Are there ways that we can use our imaginations to help us better relate to the Christmas story?

6. Have you ever noticed how many different people are included in the stories of Jesus? Who is your favorite and least favorite character in the Christmas story?

7. Like the magi, how do we look for God's miraculous workings today? Like the shepherds, how do we look for God in ordinary circumstances?

8. How is the world made a better place because of Christmas? How can we share the Christmas story with others?

Activity: Journaling

This chapter looked at the different ways that early Christians shared the stories of Jesus's birth. Can you imagine being a disciple of Jesus? How would you keep track of all the things he said and did as you journeyed with Jesus? How many things would you forget? How would you share your memories with others? What if we thought of our Gospels like journals? As you read this book, consider starting a journal to record your thoughts, prayers, and journey with Jesus.

4

Ruining Jesus's Family Tree—
Rediscovering His Adoptive Roots

Jesus had two dads. He had his heavenly Father and his earthly father.
When people see me next to my dad, it's obvious that I'm his son. As a teenager, I found this to be a bit painful. Now I just embrace it. When people look at my own children, they tend to divide them up between who looks most like my wife or like me.

Sadly, there are times when a father is unwilling to admit that he is a child's parent. This is the stuff of talk shows and tragedy. We can imagine the scene. There are multiple potential fathers present, and the audience waits for the big reveal.

Sometimes the courts have stepped in and demanded paternity tests to prove who the "real" father is. One of the most famous cases involved Steve Jobs refusing to acknowledge the legitimacy of his eldest daughter, Lisa.

When the DNA test established Jobs was her father, he initially provided $385 per month. After he became a multimillionaire, he increased this to a mere $500 per month. Over the years, his financial support increased, and in his will, Jobs provided a multimillion-dollar inheritance.[1]

A Comparison

The biological approach to paternity is often at the forefront when people read Matthew's and Luke's genealogies. People assume that Matthew and Luke are listing Jesus's genealogy because they want to demonstrate how Jesus is biologically related to King David. Thus, making him a legitimate Messiah. However, things quickly break down once the astute reader actually reads the two genealogies side-by-side and discovers that they don't quite line up.[2]

Matthew	Luke
	Adam, Seth, Enos, Cainan, Mahalaleel, Jared, Enoch, Methuselah, Lamech, Noah, Shem, Arphaxad, Cainan, Shelah, Eber, Peleg, Reu, Serug, Nahor, Terah
Abraham, Isaac, Jacob, Judah and Tamar, Perez, Hezron, Aram, *Aminadab, Nahshon,* Salmon and Rahab, *Boaz and Ruth, Obed, Jesse, David and the wife of Uriah*	*Abraham, Isaac, Jacob, Judah, Perez, Hezron,* Arni, Admin, *Aminadab, Nahshon,* Sala, *Boaz, Obed, Jesse, David*
Solomon, Rehoboam, Abijah, Asaph, Jehoshaphat, Joram, Uzziah, Jotham, Ahaz, Hezekiah, Manasseh, Amos, Josiah, Jechoniah, Salathiel	Nathan, Mattatha, Menna, Melea, Eliakim, Jonam, Joseph, Judah, Simeon, Levi, Matthat, Jorim, Eliezer, Joshua, Er, Elmadam, Cosam, Addi, Mechi, Neri, Shealtiel
Zerubbabel	*Zerubbabel*

---

1. Brennan, *Bite in the Apple*; Elkind, "When Steve Jobs' Ex-girlfriend Asked Him to Pay $25 Million for His 'Dishonorable Behavior,'" n.p.

2. I've put in italics the names that line up and reversed Luke's order. While Matthew adds the names of four women, I have included them in the names that align because their husbands are listed in Luke. Luke's listing from Adam to Terah does not necessarily conflict with Matthew since Matthew doesn't begin his genealogy until Abraham.

Matthew	Luke
Abiud, Eliakim, Azor, Zadok, Achim, Eliud, Eleazar, Matthan, Jacob	Rhesa, Joanan, Joda, Josech, Semein, Matthaias, Maath, Naggai, Esli, Nahum, Amos, Mattathias, Joseph, Jannai, Melchi, Levi, Matthat, Heli
Joseph and Mary, Jesus	*Joseph, Jesus*

Things start in relative unity from Abraham to David. However, once we reach the descendants of David, things begin to diverge more radically. Two of the most notable names show a divergence. First, Matthew 2:6 lists David's heir as Solomon, while Luke 1:31 lists Nathan. However, this isn't too big of a deal since the family trees of Solomon and Nathan reunite with Zerubbabel.

Unfortunately, the list of heirs of Zerubbabel also radically diverge and only reunite with Jesus's father, Joseph. These different lists reveal the second most significant divergence, which is that Matthew 1:16 names Joseph's father as Jacob while Luke 1:23 names him as Heli.

Can We Fix This?

So what do we make of this?

One of the most popular solutions proposes that Matthew presents the line of Joseph, while Luke presents the line of Mary.[3] The evidence comes from reading Luke 3:23, which says, "He was the son, *so it was thought*, of Joseph," to mean that Luke is actually, "wink, wink," giving the lineage of Mary.[4]

Unfortunately, such an interpretation smacks up against the plain reading of the text. In the genealogy, Luke mentions Joseph but not Mary (Luke 3:23), and he presents a male-orientated lineage for Jesus. Later, Luke

3. This view is attributed to Annius of Viterbo (about AD 1490). Conversely, Tertullian (*On the Flesh of Christ* 20; about AD 203–206) argued that Matthew gives Mary's ancestry and Luke gives Joseph's ancestry. See Huffmann, "Genealogy," 253–58.

4. This verse could be translated as "Jesus who was son (as was thought) of Joseph son of Heli," which implies a connection to Joseph as the father. Or "Jesus who was son (as was thought of Joseph) of Heli," which could imply that Heli, possibly Mary's dad, was the grandfather of Jesus.

describes Joseph as Jesus's father (Luke 4:22). So, it is most natural to understand this as Jesus's lineage through Joseph.

Further, Luke has already distinguished between the heritages of Joseph and Mary. On the one hand, he notes that Joseph comes from the house of David, which is the tribe of Judah (Luke 1:27; 2:4). On the other hand, Mary is presented as a descendant of Aaron and the tribe of Levi via her relationship with Elizabeth (Luke 1:5, 36). Because Jesus's genealogy goes through David, it must be associated with Joseph. Through Joseph and Mary's distinct lineages, Luke may want to show Jesus's unique qualifications as both king (via Joseph) and priest (via Mary).[5]

As a counterargument, some have claimed that Luke does not directly mention Mary's name in the genealogy because men would not include women in their genealogies in the first century. Thus, one rabbi notes, "The family of the father is regarded as the proper family, but the family of the mother is not regarded as proper family" (*Babylonian Talmud Baba Bathra* 109b).[6]

However, Luke is not concerned with traditional gender biases as demonstrated in the rest of his Gospel. In fact, Luke is known for challenging these biases. Throughout his Gospel, Luke highlights the roles of women such as naming Jesus's female patrons—Mary Magdalene, Joanna, and Susanna (Luke 8:1–3). So, Mary's omission from the genealogy would be uncharacteristic of Luke. More significantly, Matthew's genealogy gives evidence that women can be included in genealogies. Matthew includes Mary and four other women. If Matthew could include Mary and women in his genealogy, then so could Luke.

Wonder Women

So why does Matthew make a point of including Mary and four other women? First, his choice should remind us of all the brave women in history who have taken the lead in fighting for women's rights. But to answer this question more completely, we have to look a little closer at each woman's

---

5. Luke would not be alone in emphasizing these dual qualifications. Hebrews also highlights Jesus as both king and priest drawing upon Ps 110.

6. More importantly, genealogies were typically traced through men, not women in this period, so tracing a genealogy solely through Mary would have been unusual. See Brown, *Birth of the Messiah*, 89.

story. Each woman is identified either as a foreigner or connected with questionable sexual behavior.

First, we meet Tamar the Canaanite (Matthew 1:3; Genesis 38). She dressed up as a prostitute in order to trick her father-in-law, Judah, to sleep with her. When Judah discovers that she is pregnant, he accuses her of being a harlot. (Never mind his own hypocrisy of sleeping with prostitutes.) She counters him when she reveals that the child is *his*! (Who said the Bible was boring?) Tamar's story provides an important challenge to the sexual exploitation of women that remains relevant today. It also challenges double-standards applied to the sexual behaviors of men and women.

The second woman, Rahab (Matthew 1:5; Joshua 2), *was* a Canaanite prostitute. She protected the Israelite spies prior to Israel's conquest of Jericho. Rahab's story is a helpful reminder to the church about the importance of reaching out with God's love to those in the sex industry and offering the hope of a redeemed future.

Third, Ruth (Matthew 1:5; Ruth 3) was a Moabite immigrant widow. She convinces Boaz to marry her and provide an heir. However, her visiting Boaz in the middle of the night would have raised eyebrows. Ruth's story demonstrates God's heart for immigrants and widows.

Fourth, Matthew indirectly identifies Bathsheba as "the wife of Uriah the Hittite" (Matthew 1:6; 2 Samuel 11–12). David committed adultery with Bathsheba and murdered her husband. Bathsheba's story warns us of the dangers of powerful men.

Women in the ancient world were some of the most vulnerable members of society. All four of these women experienced further vulnerability because of their foreign connections. Yet God chose to include them, not only among his people, but within the most important lineage of all time.

In addition, these women are associated with non-Jewish people groups that were traditionally enemies of Israel. By joining these opposing ethnic groups into the Messiah's family, Matthew illustrates God's desire for racial reconciliation and for people to treat "others" as family.

Finally, Matthew includes Jesus's mother, Mary (Matthew 1:16). Matthew appears to be putting Mary in the company of women who are "shameful" either because of their foreign blood or questionable sexual behavior. Of course, Mary has not behaved badly. However, outsiders would have seen her unforeseen pregnancy as shameful. Matthew seems to be making the point that just like these women, Mary's perceived shame would be vindicated by God.

Matthew's genealogy causes us to ask some tough questions. How do we deal with things like teenage pregnancies? How do we address prostitution? Are we challenging the sexual exploitation of women by men? How do we handle the death of spouses? What about adultery? How do we help the poor, the widows, and the foreigners? Are we doing what we can, not just to help the vulnerable, but to make them part of our families? Are we part of a group of people that pours shame upon others, or do we treat people with dignity and respect? Do we contribute to a system that exploits others or brings security and safety to the most vulnerable?

Like Jesus's family tree, our families are not perfect. Sometimes the family systems we are born into, sometimes our past and current lives, and sometimes our relationships are filled with broken pieces. Sometimes there are circumstances that are hard to fix. Some can never be fixed. However, Jesus's family tree shows us that we don't have to be ashamed of our past, and that God can redeem the broken pieces and make right the injustices of our world. If God could leverage the broken and bad pieces of Jesus's family system for his greater good, can we trust him to do that for us today?

Boys Behaving Badly

However, we need to be clear that it's not just the women in this tree who were suspected of questionable behavior. Ironically, many men on this list are lifted up by faith communities for their godly behavior, but a closer examination of their lives reveals significant mistakes.

After Abraham fathered Isaac, he kicked out his African slave Hagar and his firstborn son, Ishmael (Genesis 21). Among his many misadventures, Jacob stole his brother's birthright (Genesis 27) and put his wives in a birthing competition (Genesis 29–30). We've already noted how neither Judah nor David was a saint. Solomon and many of the kings of Israel introduced the worship of foreign gods (1 Kings 11:1–13). Each of these men used his power and position for his own advantage. Of course, we could go on, but the point is that God uses flawed people.

Many of those in the genealogy made huge mistakes, and yet God still used them. Some even appear in the so-called "hall of faith" list of Hebrews 11. The point is that God can use anyone no matter what. This should be an encouragement to any reader. Regardless of what anyone has done or what has happened in our lives, no one is beyond the love of God. God can and will use anyone. We are accountable for our mistakes, but our past mistakes don't have to define us. Instead, serving God defines us.

Genealogy as Theology

Looking more closely at Mary and her fellow women in Matthew's genealogy has proven both challenging and convicting. Since Matthew has mentioned Mary, it becomes surprising that Luke does not. If we're honest with ourselves, the whole reason that we look for Mary behind Luke's list is that we are looking for a reason to explain the different names, not because Luke tells us to look for her.

Once we accept the plain reading of Luke's genealogy, we are left to conclude that both Luke and Matthew are relating Jesus's genealogy via Joseph. The next step is to attempt to explain the differences. For some, the easiest solution is just to accept that these lists are different and move on. However, a more fruitful avenue reads these lists as intentional schemas that provide "theological instruction."

What do we mean by "theological instruction"? "Theology" refers to what we think about God and God's relationship to the world. Or to put it more simply, "theology" is "God talk." By "instruction" we mean that Matthew and Luke are using these lists to tell us something about God. Unfortunately, we might miss what they are trying to teach us if we get too focused upon modern questions of biology.

We can see the theological motivations of Matthew and Luke by looking at the final person to whom Jesus's lineage is traced. Matthew begins with Abraham, the father and founder of the Israelite nation (Genesis 12–25), and he ends with Jesus. Matthew demonstrates that Jesus is a true Israelite. Luke reverses the order. He begins with Jesus and ends with the first human, Adam (Genesis 2–3). Luke demonstrates that Jesus is the savior of all humanity and undoes the sin of Adam (Romans 5:12–21).[7]

Recalling the story of Adam and Eve can be helpful. We named our youngest daughter "Eden," which means "delight," to remind ourselves of their story and the creation of the whole world (Genesis 1–2).[8] Whenever

---

7. Brown (*Birth of the Messiah*, 94) makes a similar argument that the point of the lineage is that Jesus is the son of Abraham in Matthew and the Son of God in Luke.

8. This definition for "Eden" (Hebrew, *ēden*) understands this as a cognate of the Aramaic *dn* meaning "luxury, abundance, delight, or lushness." Alternative theories argue that it is a cognate of the Sumerian *eden* meaning "plain, steppe" (Wallace, "Eden," 2:281–82).

we say her name, we have the opportunity to remember that there was a time and place where God spent his time with humanity. We remember that there was a time when God took garden walks with people. We remember how God made the world "good" (Genesis 1:4, 10, 12, 18, 21 25, 31). We also remember how the first human couple screwed up when they chose to "be like God" rather than to "be with God" (Genesis 3). In remembering the stories of creation, we also look forward to the new creation when God will redeem not just humanity but the whole world (Romans 8; Revelation 21–22).

Further, both genealogies have an organizational structure. Matthew 1:17 says that Jesus's family tree consists of three sets of fourteen. Ancient writers liked to play with numbers. Most scholars note that the number fourteen corresponds to the numeric value of David's Hebrew name, *DVD* (Hebrew only uses consonants). *D* equals four, and *V* equals six. So, four (*D*) plus six (*V*) plus four (*D*) totals fourteen.[9] Another possible explanation is that the number seven holds special value for the Jewish people. Think, for example, about the seven days in the week of creation (Genesis 1). Matthew, who likes to double things, simply doubles the number seven.[10]

While not as obvious, Luke appears to play with the number seven in a slightly different fashion by putting together a list of seventy-seven names in eleven sets of seven.[11] These eleven sets of seven generations may also be part of a twelve-week schema of world history as in other Jewish texts. For example, 4 Erza 14:11 writes, "The age is divided into twelve parts." Other writings divided history into various epics including a ten-week period (1 Enoch 93) and a thirteen-week period (2 Baruch 53–74). For Luke, Jesus is located in the climactic "eleventh week" before the end of ages.

Thus, we know by looking at the order and number of names chosen that both Matthew and Luke have made intentional decisions about whom to put on their lists. Further, anyone who has ever worked on a family tree

9. There are a couple of challenges to this schema. First, there are a couple of ways to spell David's name in the Hebrew Bible, *dāwid* and *dāwîd*, which add up to different numbers. Second, Matthew's lists don't actually add up to three sets of fourteen. If we don't repeat names, then the first group may be fourteen, the second as fourteen, and the third as thirteen. If we accept the repeated names, then the first group is fourteen, the second is fifteen, and the third is fourteen. See the discussion in Johnson, *Purpose of Biblical Genealogies*, 223–25; Hagner, *Matthew*, 1:5–7. See also Box, "Gospel Narratives of the Nativity," 80–101.

10. Examples of Matthew's doubling include two Gadarene demoniacs (Matthew 8:28), two blind men (Matthew 20:29–34), and two donkeys (Matthew 21:2).

11. Nolland, *Luke*, 1:168–69.

knows that variations are possible due to various circumstances including unexpected deaths, new marriages, or people being referred to by a variety of names.

Who Was David's Son?

Let's deal with the first major variation between Matthew and Luke. Matthew lists Solomon as David's son while Luke lists Nathan. One solution has been to cite a prophecy from the prophet Jeremiah against Jehoiachin, the last reigning Judean king from Solomon's line.[12] Jeremiah 22:30 says, "None of his offspring shall succeed in sitting on the throne of David."

This prophecy has been understood to mean that Israel's Messiah cannot come from Solomon's line, so Luke chooses Nathan. Sadly, Luke doesn't cite Jeremiah, so we can't really know what was going through his mind. However, Jeremiah 22:30 does provide a plausible theological reason for Luke's decision to clearly depart from Solomon in order to show the fulfillment of a prophecy. Luke may allude to this prophecy to remind his audience that God keeps his promises despite human failures.

On the other hand, Matthew also has theological motivations. He places a greater emphasis upon Jesus's Jewish roots as the ultimate representative of Israel. Thus, he identifies Jesus as the Messiah, who is the son of David (Matthew 1:1; 20; 9:27; 12:23; 15:22; 20:30–31; 21:9, 15; 22:42). He also notes that Jesus is the son of Abraham (Matthew 1:1, 2, 17). He tries to portray Jesus as the true son of David, especially Solomon, in order to legitimize his messianic claims. He may be influenced by verses like 2 Samuel 7:16 that promise David, "Your throne shall be established forever." So, it makes sense for him to trace Jesus's genealogy through the official reigning kings of Judah.

Regardless of which lineage is followed, both writers are making theological statements through their genealogies.[13] They are not simply providing a biological list of ancestors. Luke has probably been influenced by Jeremiah 22:30, while Matthew has been more concerned with

---

12. See also Zechariah 12:12. The nation of Israel formed under King Saul (1 Samuel 9–10), but the nation split into two kingdoms when Jeroboam led a succession from Solomon's son, Rehoboam (1 Kings 12:1–19; 2 Chronicles 10:1–19). The northern kingdom was called Israel, while the southern kingdom led by the Davidic dynasty, was called Judah.

13. Explaining the theological issue is common (Bauer, "Genealogy," 299–302).

2 Samuel 7:16 and tracing the lineage through the traditional kings of Judah.[14] We should also observe that the genealogies of Luke and Matthew rejoin briefly under Zerubbabel, which at least partially undoes the distinction between Nathan and Solomon.

Both writers want us to know that Jesus's birth is connected to God's larger plan and promises. They want us to know that God keeps his word. Luke tells us that God has been working on his redemptive plan since the creation of the world, while Matthew highlights Israel's unique role in this plan of redemption. The birth of Jesus is confirmation that God is good, consistent, and keeps his word.

Who Was Jesus's Grandpa?

The second major difference deals with the identity of Jesus's grandfather. According to Matthew, Jacob is Jesus's grandfather. According to Luke, Heli is his grandfather. This second major difference is more difficult than the previously discussed difference. This means that most solutions end up being complex.

It has been popular to speculate that these two men were actually brothers, but Heli died before having children. So, Jacob married his brother's widow, and Joseph was born. This follows a tradition called the levirate marriage (Deuteronomy 25:5–10; cf. Ruth 4:1–10). Thus, Matthew gives Joseph's biological lineage—he was born to Jacob, and Luke gives his legal lineage—he was heir to Heli.[15]

Alternatively, others argue that Mary could have been an heiress, meaning she had no brothers. So her father, Heli, adopted Joseph to join their families together (Numbers 27:8–11). Others argue that these lists refer to the same people but use different parts of their given names. Additionally, some speculate that generations are skipped allowing different men to be named. It is also possible that these genealogies reflect the

14. It is also possible that Matthew includes Solomon because one of his major themes involves comparing Jesus with Solomon. Witherington (*Matthew*, 15–21) highlights the comparison with Solomon in his commentary.

15. Thus, Julius Africanus (AD 170–245) proposed (Eusebius, *Church History* 1.7). Others reverse the lists—Matthew gives the legal lineage while Luke gives the natural lineage.

ancient practice of linking people to a common ancestor in order to express a newly created union between different groups.[16]

Ultimately, we may not be able to fully resolve the differences in these lists in a way that satisfies everyone. Although we cannot completely delve into the minds of these biblical authors, we don't want to miss the larger point that both Matthew and Luke make, which is that Jesus is Joseph's son.

The Adopted Kid

But why bother with Joseph's genealogy since he is not Jesus's biological father? Often, when we think of family, we think of genetics. But there is a whole other story to what makes up a family.

My oldest cousin is one of the most outgoing people I know. She does so much to bring our family together, including hosting occasional family gatherings. When I think of my cousin, I would tell you she's a Toney. I see her as my blood relative even though there is not a drop of my uncle's or aunt's blood in her because she was adopted.

When she was adopted, she fully and legally became a Toney. When my grandparents died, she was included in the will as the oldest grandchild. She participates in the full legacy of what it means to be a Toney because she is a Toney.

In the ancient world, adoption functioned in a similar fashion. In Jesus's day, probably the most famous adoption was when Julius Caesar adopted his grandnephew, Gaius Octavius, in 45 BC. Octavius is better known to us as Augustus Caesar.[17] Augustus's adoption as Julius's son helped him to secure his rule of the Roman Empire.

When Julius died, the Roman Senate proclaimed that he became a god at his death in 44 BC. A comet that appeared for seven days during this period was seen as confirmation of his deification (Ovid, *Metamorphosis* 15.745–851).[18] Because Julius was a god, Augustus understood himself to

---

16. This could be like the joining of Samuel's Levitical genealogy in 1 Chronicles 6:27–28, 33–34, and the Ephraimic genealogy in 1 Samuel 1:1.

17. For more on Augustus, see Jones, *Augustus*; Potter, "Augustus (Emperor)," 1:524–28; Martin and Toney, *New Testament Foundations*, 105–107.

18. Additional references to this event include Pliny the Elder, *Natural Histories* 2.23.94; Suetonius, *Divus Julius* 88; Dio Cassius 45.6.4–7; Virgil, *Eclogue* 9.47, etc.

be the "Son of God." As the "Son of God," Augustus could appeal to the gods on behalf of his subjects.[19]

This set the pattern for future Roman emperors whose predecessors were deified so that they could assume the title "Son of God" (Latin, *Divi filus*). This was so important that the Roman emperors would mint coins that inscribed "Son of God" as one of their titles so that the whole empire knew this identity.

When we look at these genealogies from the perspective of adoption, we discover that both Matthew and Luke are making the same point. Joseph adopted Jesus in order to establish his identity within Joseph's clan, as the son of David.

In fact, through naming Jesus (Matthew 1:25), Matthew highlights the legal adoption of Jesus.[20] Being adopted gave Jesus the full status and privilege of being part of Joseph's family. At the heart of the birth story is a story of adoption. For anyone considering adoption, Jesus knows what it's like to be adopted into a family. For anyone who is adopted, remember that Jesus was adopted too.

A Brand-New Family

The Gospel of John promotes images of Christians being adopted children of God. However, it makes a distinction between Jesus and believers with specific vocabulary. Jesus is the only begotten, true "Son" (Greek, *hyios*) of God (John 3:16), while believers are called "children" (Greek, *tekna*) of God (John 1:12–13).

Likewise, the apostle Paul extends the story of adoption into the Christian life. Paul makes note that Jesus was the true heir of Abraham (Galatians 3:16). Believers enjoy the privileges of the promises made to Abraham's family by being adopted into his family via faith in Jesus (Galatians 3:29). What's amazing about Christianity is that people from all different walks of life are united together as one family (Galatians 3:28–29).

We have the hope that people who are racially and ethnically different, socioeconomically different, and politically different can find unity in Christ

19. This comet was called the "Julian Star" (Latin, *Sidus Iulium*) or "Star of Caesar" (Latin, *Caesaris astrum*). For a discussion of the relationship between Augustus, Julius, and this comet, see Ramsey and Licht, *Comet of 44 B.C. and Caesar's Funeral Games*; Pandey, "Caesar's Comet," 405–49.

20. Knobloch, "Adoption," 1:78–79.

through adoption. Paul describes the power of adoption in this way, "God destined us for adoption as his children through Jesus Christ, according to the good pleasure of his will" (Ephesians 1:5). Did you catch the tail end of that quote? God derives *pleasure* from our adoption.

Elsewhere, Paul writes, "And because you are children, God has sent the Spirit of his Son into our hearts, crying, 'Abba! Father!'" (Galatians 4:6). We need to take a moment and clear up the popular misconception that *Abba* is the Aramaic word for "daddy." *Abba* simply means "father." We know this because Paul (like the similar passage in Mark 14:36) follows the normal practice of placing the translation of foreign words after the foreign word (like the translation of Jesus's last words on the cross in Mark 15:34).[21] Both Paul and Mark first transliterate the Aramaic, *Abba*, and then explain this word's meaning using the Greek word for "father" (Greek, *patēr*). They do not use the Greek word for "papa, daddy" (Greek, *pappas*). So, a clearer translation of this passage would be "Abba, which means Father."[22]

The religious leaders don't get mad at Jesus for calling God his Father. In fact, the Jewish people had a robust understanding of God as their Father (Psalms 68:5; 89:26). The religious leaders get mad because Jesus claims that while God *is* his Father, he *is not* their Father (John 8:42–45)! According to Jesus, the only way to become a child of God was through him.

What an amazing claim that followers of Jesus become children of the God of the universe! God cares for his people like a father cares for his children. For those of us with positive role models of fathers, we are challenged to think about how God exceeds our expectations. For those of us with negative role models of fathers, we are invited to be healed by God filling the void in the areas where our parents have failed.

But we shouldn't fall into the trap of thinking of God as our Father in individualistic terms. We're now part of something bigger. We're part of a new network, a new community, a new family. The message of the New Testament is that we have joined one gigantic family. We need to treat each other like family members. Look around your church, and you'll see a room full of cousins, aunts, uncles, brothers, sisters, moms, dads, and grandparents. There shouldn't be any single, unconnected people in the church.

---

21. "'Eloi, Eloi, lema sabachthani?' which means, 'My God, my God, why have you forsaken me?'" (Mark 15:34).

22. Jeremias (*Prayers of Jesus*, 11–65) originally advanced this theory, but he is rebutted by Barr ("'*Abbā* Isn't Daddy," 28–47).

Further, all previous loyalties and family identities don't matter because we have been adopted into God's family.

Christmas is the ultimate adoption story.

Reflection Questions

1. Who do you most look like or act like in your family? Are there personality traits that you're most proud of? Least proud of? Do you imagine that Jesus would have looked like Mary? Did he learn any personality traits from his parents?

2. Why do you think Matthew and Luke have different genealogies? What do you think are the best explanations for the differences?

3. What do the genealogies teach us about God's plans and his abilities to keep his promises?

4. What do these genealogies teach us about the importance of legacy and families? What kind of legacy do you hope to leave behind?

5. What lessons do we learn from Tamar, Rahab, Ruth, Bathsheba, and Mary? Do they teach us anything about being mothers? How can we imitate their examples? These women also raise a series of complex questions such as how do we address prostitution (Tamar and Rahab)? How do we address sexual exploitation and adultery (Bathsheba)? How do we help the poor, widows, and foreigners (Ruth)? How do we deal with teenage pregnancies (Mary)?

6. How do we understand the complexity of the men in the genealogies who are understood to be both godly and also who made significant mistakes? Why do you think these lists mainly focus on the men? Do they teach us anything about being fathers?

7. Matthew and Luke teach about the virgin birth, so why do they give Joseph's genealogy?

8. Looking at Jesus's birth stories, what lessons do we learn about the importance of adoption? How can we follow Joseph's example of adopting Jesus? What does it mean for Christians to be adopted into God's family?

Activity: *Lectio Divina*

Let's return to the story of Jesus's birth and reflect upon Matthew's version of the story. *Lectio Divina* (Latin for "Divine Reading") is another form of Scripture reading that invites us to slow down and listen for the still, small voice of God to speak to us through his Word. It includes four movements. First, calm your mind through a slow and gradual reading of Matthew 1:18–25. Second, listen for God's voice in the passage by focusing on a particular word, phrase, image, and so forth. Third, read and pray through the passage, and try to make it a conversation with God. Finally, take a few moments of silence, trying to listen as you contemplate the passage.

5

Ruining Jesus's Name—Rediscovering the Power of His Name

H is name wasn't "Jesus."

All my life I've known that I shared my name with a ranch hand who worked on my grandfather's farm. In my room hung a little plaque with a duck and the definition, "Carl means strong," along with the Bible verse, "Finally, be strong in the Lord and in the strength of his power" (Ephesians 6:10). Now I have to tell you that if you met me in person, my five-foot, eight-inch frame would not strike you as particularly "strong." But my parents would tell you that I'm at least strong-willed.

Anyone who picks up a book of baby names quickly learns that the path toward understanding a person's name involves knowing what language and culture the name came from. My name originated in Norway and Sweden and is a name of royalty. Sadly, I don't have any kingly blood flowing through my veins. Some famous (or infamous) Carls have included

57

Carl Jung, the psychologist, Carl Sagan, the astronomer, Carl Lewis, the Olympic gold runner, Carl Henry, the founding editor of *Christianity Today*, and Carl Karcher, the founder of Carl's Jr. restaurants.

Like many names, my name has a variety of spellings, depending on the country. There is the Germanic spelling of "Karl," which always seemed to be much easier to find at novelty shops that had names on things like mugs or bicycle license plates. Notable Karls include the theologian, Karl Barth, and the communist, Karl Marx. The Spanish variant of "Carlos" yields a whole slew of famous people. My favorite people who share my namesake are guitarist Carlos Santana and Carlos Ray Norris (a.k.a. Chuck Norris).

Your Name Means What!

In the case of the name "Jesus," it is important to understand a bit about the original languages of our Bible. What Christians call the "Old Testament" (but Jewish people simply call Scripture) was primarily written in Hebrew (with a little bit of Aramaic). However, the "New Testament" was written in Greek.

For some biblical characters, their names mean something. So, we are told that "Esau" was named because he was "red" and "hairy" (Genesis 25:25).[1] His twin brother, "Jacob," which means "supplanter" (Genesis 25:26), got his name because he held onto his brother's heel.[2] Later, Jacob was given the name "Israel," which means "one who contends with God" (Genesis 32:28) because he wrestled with an angel of God.

As the founding father of the nation of Israel, God renamed "Abram," meaning "exalted ancestor," to "Abraham," which means "ancestor of a multitude" (Genesis 17:5).[3] We are told that "Moses" means "drawn out from the water" (Exodus 2:10) because he was taken out of the Nile River by a princess.[4] The book of Isaiah includes a whole series of names that have

1. "Red" is related to Edom, and "hairy" is related to Seir.

2. Jacob's name is associated with "heel" (Genesis 25:26) and "cheat" (Genesis 27:36). It may also be the shortened form of the Hebrew word for "God protects."

3. The popular view that God renamed "Saul" as "Paul" on the Damascus road projects this notion of God renaming significant figures. However, this view is wrong. "Saul" is simply his Jewish name while "Paul" is his Greek name (see Acts 13:9). Acts continues to use "Saul" after the Damascus Road and only switches during Paul's first missionary journey.

4. While the biblical text gives a popular meaning for the name of Moses, the name

significance. Less fortunate names include the longest personal name in the Bible, "Maher-shalah-hash-baz," meaning "quick to the plunder, swift to the spoil" (Isaiah 8:1). I think I'd just call him "Baz."

What we learn from the Bible is that names often give people an identity and have significance. What we call ourselves and what we call others matters. We get this concept when we teach our kids not to make fun of others by name-calling. We get this when we come up with nicknames for people. So what names are we calling ourselves in our private thoughts? Do we call ourselves a loser? Unattractive? Unlovable? Popular? Smart? Articulate?

What is our identity rooted in? The Bible calls us to find our identity, not in the labels we put upon ourselves but "in Christ." The most powerful symbol of this imagery comes from Christian baptism where believers are described as dying to their old selves by identifying with Jesus's death and experiencing new life through his resurrection (Romans 6). Paul also uses the image of the "body of Christ" to describe both the differences and unity that Christians experience (Romans 12:4–8; 1 Corinthians 12:12–31).

"In Christ," we followers of Jesus can die to our bad thoughts and behaviors and find ourselves alive to God (Romans 6:11). Further, "in Christ" we also don't have to remain condemned by our past (Romans 8:1). Instead, "in Christ" we are new people (2 Corinthians 5:17). "In Christ," we are put in right relationship with God and others (Galatians 2:16).

"In Christ," nothing can separate us from God's love (Romans 8:39). "In Christ," we are not alone; we join God's people, are made part of God's family, and become heirs to God's promises (Galatians 3:14, 26, 29). "In Christ," racism, sexism, and elitism are all abolished because we are all the same (Galatians 3:28). "In Christ," we are blessed with spiritual blessings (Ephesians 1:3). "In Christ," we have a future since we are promised eternal life (Romans 6:23; 1 Corinthians 15:22).

Being "in Christ" means that our new identity is tied to Jesus's reputation. We understand what it means to have our reputation tied to a larger group or person. For example, sports fans get associated with their teams. What kind of people do you associate with the Las Vegas Raiders, Green Bay Packers, Chicago Bears, or San Francisco 49ers? Similarly, college students get associated with their universities. We sense the difference between saying that we went to community college versus going to Harvard.

---

also derives from the Egyptian *msy*, which means "to give birth." See Beegle, "Moses (Person)," 4:911.

Likewise, people can be identified by their political parties. What comes to mind when we think of a Democrat, Republican, or Independent?

So what about you? Are you religious? What is the reputation of the church in our society today? What is the reputation of being a Christian? Is it possible that we need to realign our reputations to ground our identity in Jesus rather than ourselves? Christmas offers us a chance of rebirth and reinvention. We can come to the manger, worship the king, and find our identity in Christ.

Lord Help Me!

In the Bible, names also hold power. If you knew the name of your god, then you had access to that god's power. You might even be able to control that god. So, it's really significant when Israel's God revealed to Moses that his name is Yahweh, which means "I am who I am" (Exodus 3:14). This name may be understood as a fundamental description of God's existence—"I exist." It may also be a statement that God is the creator—"I bring into being." But I prefer understanding this name as a promise that God will remain present with his people—"I will be with you."[5]

God's name is so powerful and precious that one of the Ten Commands is "You shall not make wrongful use of the name of the LORD your God, for the LORD will not acquit anyone who misuses his name" (Exodus 20:7). Sadly, people sometimes have interpreted this command as merely an avoidance of using "God" or "Jesus" as a swearword.

But "misuse" is more than cursing. Misuse also involves issues of reverence and respect. If you spoke with a practicing Jewish person, he or she would avoid saying the name of God. Instead, he or she would say "*Ha Shem*," which means "the Name," or "*Adonai*," which means "Lord." Following this practice, many English Bible translations write "LORD" in all capitals to translate the name of God in the Old Testament.

Ironically, the name "Jehovah" was created by Christians who misread the name of God in rabbinical copies of the Old Testament.[6] So how did this happen? It turns out that Hebrew words only use consonants. So, "Yahweh" in the Hebrew Bible would look something like this: יהוה.

---

5. Seow, "God, Names of," 2:590.

6. Based on the 1530 translation of William Tyndale of Exodus 6:3, the 1611 King James Version uses the name Jehovah in its translation of Exodus 6:3, Psalm 83:18; and Isaiah 12:2; 26:4, but the New King James Version no longer uses this word.

Transliterating this word into current English letters looks like this: *YHWH*, and the earlier transliteration looked like this: *JHVH*. Latter rabbis added vowels to aid in pronunciation. Because the rabbis wanted to remind their readers to say *"Adonai"* (English "Lord") instead of God's name, they inserted the vowels of *Adonai* (a/e, o, ai/a) whenever they copied the name of God. So, they wrote *"JeHoVaH."*

Sadly, the name Jehovah is just a made-up word that represents a Western misunderstanding of a Middle Eastern culture. Every time I hear the name "Jehovah," I am reminded of the importance of listening and learning from other cultures rather than projecting my own assumptions and values upon others. When I pay attention to Jewish culture, one of the things that I learn is the value of respect. From this perspective, one way to respect God is not to say his name.

We can contrast this sense of respect with contemporary Christian practices like worship songs or prayers where people constantly say God's name. For Christians, we do this because it evokes a sense of intimacy. We tend to dispense with formality because it feels like "legalism" or too much like a "religion" instead of a "relationship."

But there is wisdom in showing respect for the name of God. As Christians, we describe God as our "Father." Because of this, I can't help but think of my relationship with my kids. I've got four children. At some point while growing up, every one of them figured out that my name is "Carl." And every one of them has called me "Carl" instead of "dad." (Usually with a little smile or smirk on their face.)

Now I understand that we all have different parenting practices, so I'm not trying to judge anyone who raises their kids differently. But in those moments, when my son or daughter has called me "Carl," I have gotten down on my knees so that I could look him or her in the eyes. Then, I would say (with my own smile), "Everyone in the whole world gets to call me 'Carl.' But only you and your brothers and sisters get to call me 'dad.'"

Like my kids, we've all learned God's name, and some of us really like to say it. Still, I think there is something more intimate and personal that occurs when we don't use God's name but instead call him "Father." As our Father, God will never stop caring for us. He will never walk away. He is always with us. He desires to be close with us. He always wants the best for us.

Equally, I think there is something intimate, personal, and appropriate when we call our sibling Jesus by his personal name. It's amazing to think that we have been invited to join the family of God. It's also exciting to know that we are not joining some exclusive, closed family. Just as we are encouraged to join the family of God, the invitation is open to anyone in our lives. Our friends, neighbors, and families can all be part of this massive family. We can all find a place called home. We can all find a place to belong.

Saving Jesus's Name

In the New Testament, we are introduced to Mary and Joseph's child whom they named "Jesus." The name "Jesus" is the English translation of the Greek name *Iēsous* (pronounced Ee-ay-souce[7]).

"Jesus" (*Iēsous*) was the name that many of the first Christians called their savior. However, it wasn't the name that was given to him by his parents or the name that his friends and disciples called him.[8] If you called out "*Iēsous*" to him from across a village square, he wouldn't turn his head because he wouldn't know you were talking to him. This is because Jesus, as a first-century Jew, was given the Hebrew name "*Yeshua*" (pronounced Yay-shoo-ah[9]), which our New Testament writers translate for us into Greek.

The name *Yeshua* was created by joining parts of two words together. *Ye* is the first part of God's name, "Yahweh," and *shua* means "saves." So, the name *Yeshua* means "Yahweh saves." We see Matthew's Gospel highlighting this connection between the name of Jesus and the meaning of salvation when he writes, "You are to name him Jesus, for he will save his people from their sins" (Matthew 1:21).

That means that every time a person says the name of "Jesus," we are making a declaration that God saves. We might even say that Jesus's name is shorthand for the gospel promise—God saves. When Christians close their prayers in "Jesus's name" (John 14:13–14), we end with a reminder of a promise from God that he saves.[10]

So the next time you tell God about your troubles, and you close your prayers with "in Jesus's name," remember that you are handing those problems over to God. In his wisdom, he will lead you on a path that

---

7. "I" as in aud*i*ence, "e" as in ob*e*y, and "ou" as in s*ou*p.

8. Meyer, "Jesus (Person)," 3:773–96.

9. "E" as in b*e*t, "u" as in r*u*e, "a" as in ban*a*na.

10. Praying in Jesus's name is an important theme in the farewell discourse of John (15:7, 16; 16:23–24, 26; cf. 1 John 3:22; 5:14–15). One of the major themes of the book of Acts is the power of Jesus's name (Acts 2:38; 3:6, 16; 4:10, 12, 17–18, 30; 5:28, 40–41; 8:12, 16; 9:16, 21, 27, 28; 10:48; 15:26; 16:18; 19:5, 13, 17; 21:13; 22:16; 26:9).

saves you from those problems. He will either give you the strength to endure them or to overcome them. When you thank God for the blessings in your life, and you conclude with "in Jesus's name," you can remind yourself that those blessings come from a gracious God. When you pray for others, and you end "in Jesus's name," you are entrusting your loved ones into the hands of God.

Meet My Boy "Josh"

Let's connect this Jewish name to a biblical character in our English Bibles. Was Jesus named after anyone? It turns out that *Yeshua* is a form of the name *Yehoshua* (Nehemiah 8:17). Great. So who's *Yehoshua*? In the Old Testament, *Yehoshua* is "Joshua" (Exodus 17:9; 24:13; 33:11; etc.). "Jesus" (a.k.a. "Joshua") was named after *the* Joshua whose stories were so epic that he has a book of the Bible named after him. Joshua's stories focused on bringing God's people into the land that he had promised their ancestors (Genesis 12, 15, 17).

Under Moses, God delivered his people from the Egyptians (Exodus 1–15), made a covenant with them with the Ten Commandments and Law (Exodus 20–24), and dwelt among them with his tabernacle, which was a fancy tent (Exodus 25–40).

Despite all these great acts of God, the Israelites didn't fully trust him when they had the chance to enter the Promised Land. When they looked upon the inhabitants of the land, they were filled with fear. The task seemed too hard. So, God didn't let them in. Instead, God hit a big "reset-button" by making the people wait forty years so that the unbelieving generation would die off, and their kids could have a second chance to enter into the Promised Land (Numbers 13–14).

This story is a good reminder that God doesn't punish children for their parents' mistakes (Deuteronomy 24:16; Ezekiel 18). Likewise, Jesus taught this principle when he healed the blind man (John 9:1–7.)

With Joshua, God made good on his promises to Israel, beginning with crossing the Jordan River (Joshua 3–4) and taking the land (Joshua 1, 5–24). Similarly, we see Jesus's ministry beginning with a metaphorical Jordan River "crossing" through his baptism by John the Baptist (Matthew 3:13–17; Mark 1:9–11; Luke 3:21–22; John 1:29–34). Then, Jesus endures forty days in the desert (Matthew 4:1–11; Mark 1:12–13; Luke 4:1–13), which parallels the forty years of Israel's wilderness wanderings.[11]

Many readers have noticed the parallels between Jesus's three temptations by Satan in the wilderness and the temptations that the people of Israel faced while in the desert.[12] The first temptation for Jesus to turn stones into bread parallels the Israelites' complaint about no food (Exodus 16, Numbers 11). Jesus responds to the Devil by saying that a person will not live by bread alone (Deuteronomy 8:3). The next temptation to jump to his death and let God save him connects to the Israelites' continual testing of God in the wilderness. Jesus replies with a reminder not to put God to the test (Deuteronomy 6:16). The other temptation to worship the Devil parallels the idolatry of the golden calf (Exodus 32). Jesus responds by declaring that people should worship God alone (Deuteronomy 6:13). In telling these temptation stories, Matthew and Luke demonstrate the idea that where Israel failed, their Messiah, Jesus, has triumphed.

After Jesus's Jordan River crossing and triumph over the Devil in the desert, he reenters the land and calls twelve disciples (Matthew 10:1–4; Mark 3:13–19; Luke 6:12–16). These twelve disciples represent the twelve tribes of Israel. Jesus then goes through the land of Israel "conquering" the spiritual foes of demonic forces through exorcisms, and he heals people in the land of illnesses.

Even today, Jesus, like Joshua, is still fighting for us. He doesn't surrender. He's on our side. Even when we don't think he is fighting for us, he is still fighting. Jesus won't abandon us to the forces of sin and death in this world. How often do we forget that Jesus has our back? We may feel overwhelmed by the onslaught of life. Like in 2020, when we experienced the coronavirus pandemic shutting down the entire world. Or when we heard the cries of injustice filling the streets over the police killing Black people. Or when the western United States was engulfed in flames. Or when murder hornets arrived in the state of Washington. So where do we need Jesus's help today? Breathe. Then remember that Jesus is on our side.

---

11. N. T. Wright (*New Testament and People of God; Jesus and the Victory of God*) is one of the leading scholars to develop exodus motifs in Jesus's ministry and how he rehearses the stories of Israel. See also, Martin and Toney, *New Testament Foundations*, 237.

12. The last two temptations are in a different order in Luke. Matthew moves from the lower desert to the higher pinnacle of the temple to the highest mountain. There is a similar story of a contest between Abraham and the Devil in *the Babylonian Talmud Sanhedrin* 89b. Talbert, *Matthew*, 60–62.

Bring the Kingdom

In his ministry, Jesus called people to turn to the kingdom of God (Mark 1:15–16). This kingdom of God was not some political institution. He was not trying to overthrow the Jewish or Roman leadership. However, he did critique this leadership and challenged it to change its ways. This expression "kingdom of God" was Jesus's way of saying that God was *really* in charge.[13] He proclaimed that God was the true ruler, and he called this idea the "gospel" or "good news" (Greek, *euangelion*).

Jesus knew that the world he lived in was not quite right. He knew the people in charge were not doing a great job. So, he made the bold claim that God should be in charge of the lives of anyone who wished to submit to his rule. Jesus called his disciples to "repent," or to "change their mind" about the direction of their lives. Instead of trusting themselves or others, they were called to "believe," that is, to "trust" in God by submitting their loyalty to him.[14] Jesus challenged people to let God be in charge.

How often are we people who need a change in our mindset? Who is *really* in charge of our lives? Jesus's call to his first disciples to stop trusting in themselves or in others is a call that is still heard today. What does it mean for government and social accountability if God is ultimately in charge? What would our homes look like if God were in charge? What would our schools look like if God were in charge? What are the things that we need to entrust to God? To let him be in charge?

When the angel of the Lord tells Jesus's parents to name him "Joshua" (Matthew 1:21; Luke 2:21), they enter into the Old Testament story of salvation and remember the origin story of the nation of Israel. This origin story is what we might call the "gospel" or "good news" story of the Old Testament. It is the story of Israel's exodus from Egypt and entry into the Promised Land.

With his name, Jesus and his family were reminded on a daily basis that the story of salvation is not new, and that their God is a god who saves. Just as Israel was saved in her past from the Egyptians, so Jesus had come as the new Joshua to save Israel and all people from the forces of sin and death.

---

13. For more on the kingdom of God/kingdom of heaven expression, see Green, "Kingdom of God/Heaven," 468–81.

14. See the discussion of these terms and Jesus's gospel message in Martin and Toney, *New Testament Foundations*, 237–38. See also, Bates, *Gospel Allegiance;* McKnight, *King Jesus Gospel.*

Likewise, today, it is important to remember our history. It's important to tell the stories of God's salvation. We need to be reminded that God is in the business of saving his people. We need to be telling each other stories where we've seen God act. If God can save his people in the past, he can save his people in the future. Christmas reminds us that God sent Jesus into the world to save the world and to make things right.

All in the Family

Just as we learn a lot about the hopes and dreams of Israel from Jesus's name, we can learn even more by looking at the names of the rest of his family. We learn that they believed in the faithfulness of God. They named their children after significant people whom God used to fulfill his promises.

So, we discover Jesus's father's name was "Joseph." Joseph (*and his Amazing Technicolored Dreamcoat*) was one of the twelve sons of Jacob (Genesis 37–50). After his brothers faked his death and sold him, he was sent to Egypt where he went from house slave to prisoner to helping the pharaoh rule the land. Joseph was the first great deliverer of his family, and he saved them during a time of famine. The Gospel of Matthew draws on two significant parallels between the patriarch Joseph and Jesus's father. Both are known for receiving and interpreting dreams (Genesis 37:19), and both save their families by bringing them to Egypt (Genesis 46:2–4).[15]

His mother, "Mary," whose Hebrew name was "Miriam," was named after Moses's sister who helped lead the Israelites out of Egypt (Exodus 2, 15; Numbers 12). His brother, "James," whose Hebrew name is "Jacob," was named after the father of the twelve tribes of Israel (Genesis 25–50). Finally, we read about his brother "Jude," which is also translated into English as "Judas." However, we avoid that translation to avoid confusion with *the* Judas. Jude's Hebrew name is "Judah," and he was named after Jacob's son (Genesis 29, 35, 50). Judah's tribe included King David, from whose house the Messiah, the savior of Israel would arise.

Giving children religious names is nothing new, and it is a practice that continues today. English speakers surely know people who are named "Joseph," "Mary," "James," "Jacob," or "Jude." Likewise, in Spanish-speaking countries, we find children with a variety of religious names, including those named after Jesus's family, like his parents "José" and "María," as well as the child "Jesús."

15. Brown, *Birth of the Messiah*, 112.

For some English speakers, naming a child with the same name as the Son of God may sound sacrilegious. Still, we have just discovered through our tracing of the origins of the name of "Jesus" that anyone named "Joshua" has also been named after the same biblical figures. In fact, I think it's fun to call my friends named Josh, "Jesus."

It is fantastic that we have a world full of Joshuas and Jesúses. Every time we say those names, we are reminded of the stories of Joshua and Jesus. We can remember how God used both of these people to save others. Whenever I say the name "Joshua" or "Jesus," I am reminded that God is still in the business of salvation today and that he can use any of us today to save others.

Are we a people who look for God's salvation in our daily lives? Do we hand our problems over to him and ask him to save us? When we are confronted with problems, do we simply rely upon ourselves to fix them? Or do we ask others for help? What if we also asked God to help us?

Do we put God in charge, or are we in charge of our own destinies? When we wake up in the morning, do we set our own agendas, or do we have our agendas set for us by others? What if we began our day by asking God to set our agendas? Do we look for how God can save others? Or do we say, "God helps those who help themselves"? What if we acted like the hands and feet of Jesus and tried to help others, but also asked for God's help?

Remember, every time we say the name "Jesus," we recount the two greatest stories of salvation found in the Bible. We remember God's first great act of salvation—the exodus from Egypt and entry into the Promised Land. We also remember God's second great act of salvation—Jesus's ministry, death, and resurrection. In addition, we look forward to the third and final great act of salvation—his return.

Reflection Questions

1. Do you know what your name means? Does your name reveal anything about your personality? Was there a meaning of a name from this chapter that stuck out to you?

2. From this chapter, we learned that names in the Bible often mean something and give people an identity and have significance. What is our identity rooted in? How do we root our identity in Christ?

3. While we know Yahweh is the name of God, we also learned the importance of thinking of God as our Father. What does it mean for you to think of God as your Father? How do we help others feel part of God's family?

4. This chapter explained how the name Jehovah was a mistaken translation for the name of God based on a misunderstanding of Jewish culture. How do we improve our ability to listen to other cultures rather than projecting our own cultures and values upon others?

5. We learned that Jesus is named after Joshua, which creates links between Jesus and the Exodus story. What parallels between the Exodus story and Jesus's story did you find helpful?

6. Jesus's name means "Yahweh saves." Where do we need God's salvation today? What are some of our big and small problems? When we are confronted with these problems, do we rely upon ourselves to fix them? Do we ask others for help? How do we ask God for help?

7. What can we do to help us remember that God is in the business of saving people? Can you share with others any stories about God helping you?

8. Jesus's gospel message was to submit to the kingdom of God, which means putting God in charge. When we look around in this world, does it look like God is in charge? What would it look like for us to put God in charge of ourselves, our families, or our communities?

Activity: Remembering God's Word

This chapter explored the meaning of Jesus's name in order to remind us of God's promise to save his people. But God's promises can quickly be forgotten in the busyness of our days. We have an opportunity to listen to God's voice throughout our day by remembering God's word. Try learning the following verse: "You are to name him Jesus, for he will save his people from their sins" (Matthew 1:21). If you have trouble remembering the verse, then write it down on a piece of paper. Then, throughout the day read or recite the verse asking God to guide your paths by his word remembering that "Yahweh saves."

6

Ruining Jesus's Birth—Rediscovering the Tale of Two Virgins

U nexpected pregnancies can throw our lives off. That's a huge understatement.

I've had older friends who had basically raised their kids and then became surprised by a pregnancy. Apparently, there is nothing quite like people thinking that you're the grandparent of your own kid. Another friend got a vasectomy. Months later, he discovered that his wife was pregnant. Again, nothing like sorting through the emotions ranging from puzzlement to suspicion to excitement. Other friends have gotten pregnant in high school, and their lives were forever changed.

Even planned babies can throw life into chaos. For the birth of our first child, my father-in-law and mother-in-law came to help. Trying to juggle the "right" amount of time where they were helpful but not in the way, they planned to stay with us for two weeks arriving just a few days before the due date.

After picking them up from the airport and settling everyone in for the evening, I decided that I should take a sleeping pill to help calm my nerves and give me at least one more good night's sleep before our baby would enter our lives. It turns out that my soon-to-be-born child didn't care about my plans. Shortly after my head hit the pillow, my wife woke me up with the news that the baby was on her way! And that was how "Zoe," whose name means "life," was born.

More Sex Talk

There have been all sorts of controversy about how to understand Matthew's prophecy of the virgin birth. First off, it's important to be a little more precise in our language. Matthew 1:18–25 and Luke 1:26–38 both talk about Jesus's virginal *conception*, not necessarily a virgin birth.[1]

While I'm not a medical doctor, I know a little bit about "the birds and the bees," as well as the importance of the meaning of words. A "virgin" is simply someone who has not had sex. I've had several friends who got pregnant the first time they had sex. Technically, they were all "virgins" who became pregnant. More radical is the claim of the Gospels that Mary became pregnant without having sex with anyone. Both Matthew and Luke are clear that Joseph was not involved in creating Jesus. Thus, what Mary experienced was a virginal *conception*.

Matthew notes that "before they lived together, she was found to be with child from the Holy Spirit" (Matthew 1:18). Further, the angel tells Joseph, "The child conceived in her is from the Holy Spirit" (Matthew 1:20). And in case you missed his point, he writes that Joseph "had no martial relations with her until she had borne a son" (Matthew 1:25).

Likewise, the Gospel of Luke clearly emphasizes that Mary was a "virgin" (Greek, *parthenos*) when the angel Gabriel tells her that she will bear a son (Luke 1:27, 34). When Mary asks how this is possible, the angel explains

---

1. See the discussion of Brown, *Birth of the Messiah*, 517–31; *Virginal Conception and Bodily Resurrection of Jesus*. Interestingly, the rest of the New Testament is silent on this topic.

that "the Holy Spirit will come upon you" (Luke 1:35). So, there is no doubt that both of these Gospels clearly think that Joseph was not Jesus's biological father. Instead, the Holy Spirit was responsible for this miraculous conceptiopn that did not involve sexual intercourse. This stands in contrast with Greek and Roman stories of their gods who impregnate women.[2]

Like a Virgin?

In support of the concept of a virgin birth, Matthew 1:22–23 claims, "All this took place to fulfill what had been spoken by the Lord through the prophet: 'Look, the virgin shall conceive and bear a son, and they shall name him Emmanuel,' which means, 'God is with us.'" From these verses, Matthew clearly thinks that Jesus was born of a virgin because he uses the Greek word, *parthenos*, which means "virgin."[3]

However, all sorts of controversies have arisen when we look at the biblical prophecy that Matthew quotes in Isaiah 7:14. For some traditions, it has become a measure of Christian "orthodoxy" versus "liberalism," depending on how Bibles translate this verse.

While the Bibles you and I read are likely written in English, it is important to understand that the Old Testament and the New Testament were originally composed in different languages. We learned in our chapter about Jesus's name that the Old Testament is mainly written in Hebrew, while the New Testament was written in Greek. This is what Isaiah 7:14 looks like in these languages:

Hebrew

הָעַלְמָה הָרָה וְיֹלֶדֶת בֵּן וְקָרֵאת שְׁמוֹ עִמָּנוּ אֵל

Greek

ἡ παρθένος ἐν γαστρὶ ἕξει καὶ τέξεται υἱόν καὶ καλέσεις τὸ ὄνομα αὐτοῦ Ἐμμανουήλ

---

2. Various parallels in non-Christian literature include Dionysus by Zeus (Diodorus Siculus 4:2:1), Romulus son of Mars (Ovid, *Metamorphosis* 14:805–28; Plutarch, *Romulus* 2), Alexander the Great's conception (Plutarch, *Alexander* 2), and Plato by Apollo (Diogenes Laertius 3:2; Origen, *Against Celsus* 1:37). These parallels differ in that they almost always involve some divine male appearing as a human or another form that impregnates the woman (Davies and Allison, *Matthew* 1:214–16).

3. Any good Greek language dictionary can be used to explore these ideas. For example, see Delling, "*Parthenos*," 5:826–37.

Unless you were raised speaking those languages or were taught them, they probably looked like confusing gibberish. To make things even more confusing for English readers, Hebrew is read from right to left, while Greek is read from left to right. In addition, the original Hebrew only used consonants. All those little dots and dashes around the letters are the vowels, which were added later by scribes. Greek writers originally did not use spaces between words and used all capital letters. So using the NIV English translation, this is what the Hebrew and Greek would look like:

Hebrew

NS T HTRB VG DN VCNC LLW NGRV HT

LNMM MH LLC LLW DN

Greek

THEVIRGINWILLCONCEIVEANDGIVEBIRTHTOASO
NANDWILLCALLHIMIMMANUEL

This helps us get a little better "feel" for the challenges faced by ancient Jewish authors who translated the Old Testament from Hebrew to Greek. The Greek translation of the Old Testament is called the Septuagint. The name means "seventy" because, according to legend, there were seventy translators.[4]

Isaiah 7:14 uses the Hebrew word *almah*, which broadly means "young woman of marriageable age" (see Genesis 24:43). However, it can also more specifically mean "virgin." I like to think of *almah* as an umbrella term encompassing a variety of more specific meanings. In comparison, the different Hebrew word *bethulah* more narrowly means "virgin."[5]

Like any word, we understand a word's meaning because of context. For example, in English, if you address someone using Mr. or Ms., you do not know whether that person is single or married. In fact, before meeting my wife, I was Mr. Toney. However, if you see something like Mr. and Ms. Toney, you would know that we were a married couple. The word "Mr." didn't change, but the context did change the word's meaning from "single man" to "married man."

So when the Greek translators saw this Hebrew word, *almah*, they were given some choices as they moved this concept from one language to another. One way they translated this was the Greek word *neanis*,

4. This legend is recorded in the *Letter of Aristeas*.
5. Watts, "Excursus,"1:136–37.

which means "young woman."[6] However, the translators of the Septuagint chose the more specific Greek word *parthenos*, which means "virgin." For these Greek translators, they were not thinking of a virginal conception. Instead, they were simply thinking of a young, unmarried woman, who would have been a virgin.

Context is Queen or King!

When Matthew read his Greek Bible, he would naturally see how the "virgin" (Greek, *parthenos*) of Isaiah 7:14 perfectly described Mary's situation. But we still have to ask ourselves, what did Isaiah mean when he wrote this passage? Did he think about the future Messiah, that is, Jesus, or was something else going on?

The rules of interpretation say that context is king or queen! Taking things out of context changes meaning. For example, if you were sick, you wouldn't want your medical doctor to prescribe for you "hugs" based on the popular anti-drug slogan "Hugs not drugs."

Even using the same word does not guarantee the same meaning. For example, the English word "board" has a variety of meanings depending on the context. You can *board* a boat. Businesses often have some kind of *board* of trustees. A piece of lumber is also called a *board*. So how does the context of Isaiah help us to understand *almah*?

We discover that Isaiah 7:14 is part of a larger story begun in chapter 7. Here we encounter an ancient Israelite King named Ahaz who ruled the southern kingdom of Judah during the eighth century BC (2 Kings 16; 2 Chronicles 28). At this time, he was being attacked by two armies—one from the kingdom of Aram and the other from the northern kingdom of Israel. Being under attack and outnumbered, he was naturally worried (Isaiah 7:1–2).

God sent Isaiah the prophet to speak into this situation (Isaiah 7:3). He gave Ahaz mixed news. The good news was that Aram and Israel would soon no longer be a threat (Isaiah 7:4–9). The bad news was that an even bigger threat was coming, the kingdom of Assyria (Isaiah 7:16–25). This is almost like saying, don't worry about the wolves chasing you because pretty soon a bear will eat them.

---

6. Origin's Hexapla includes three translations by Aquila, Symmachus, and Theodotion that use *neanis*.

Now Ahaz didn't seem to believe Isaiah's prophecy claiming, "I will not put the LORD to the test" (Isaiah 7:12). But God wanted to give him a sign to prove that these words were true (Isaiah 7:10, 13). Guess what that sign was? "The virgin will conceive and give birth to a son . . . " (Isaiah 7:14 NIV). Anyone who *only* sees Jesus as this child is left with a problem. How is the birth of a child several hundred years in the future a sign for Ahaz?

Put bluntly. It isn't.

However, others retort, "How can a 'virgin' have a child? This must be Jesus!" But this misunderstands the Hebrew concept of a "virgin" or a "young woman." Anyone who hasn't had sex is a virgin. Once a virgin has sex, she can have children.[7] Isaiah was simply pointing to some unidentified young girl.[8] Then he said that she would have a kid, and this would be a sign to Ahaz.

The further objection comes from this child being called "Immanuel," which means "God is with us." People say, "Clearly this means the incarnation! Only Jesus can truly be 'God with us.'" But this expression can also be read as a broad statement of God showing up and being present with his people by saving them from their immediate enemies and bringing further judgment with the Assyrians.[9]

If we ignore the original story in Isaiah, we risk losing the lessons taught to Ahaz. The prophet Isaiah teaches Ahaz and the people of Judah that God is attentive to their problems. Even when something is as dire as two kings sitting at the city gates, God is still present and ready to deliver his people. When we have problems in life, God wants to show up.

What are the problems that we are currently facing? Do we feel like we are facing these problems alone? Do our problems feel like armies outside our city gates? What if we asked and expected God to show up in order to help us face our problems? For Christians, the Bible gives us good news. God has already shown up and is already here with us through the Holy Spirit (John 16:5–15; Romans 8:11; Galatians 3:1–5; Ephesians 1:13). We don't have to face our problems alone.

---

7. Walton ("עֲלוּמִים," 4:415–19) goes on to argue that the concept of an *almah* would extend even after the birth of a first child.

8. Watts (*Isaiah* 1:136–37, 140–42) notes that there are various proposals for the identification of the young woman including Mary, a princess, a queen, or the prophet's wife. If the young woman was a queen, then this could be Abia who becomes the mother of Hezekiah (2 Kings 18:2).

9. God promised to be with the Davidic dynasty of kings in a special way (2 Samuel 7:9; 1 Kings 1:37; 11:38; Psalm 89:22, 25). Wildberger, *Isaiah 1–12*, 293.

But Isaiah also teaches us that there is some danger when God decides to show up. Because God is both merciful and just, we have to be ready for both God's blessings and God's punishments. Ahaz didn't always trust God. In fact, Ahaz wasn't a good king. We are told he was responsible for gristly acts such as child-sacrifices in the Hinnom Valley (2 Kings 23:10; 2 Chronicles 28:3). These sacrifices were so horrifying that they are the background of Jesus's image of Gehenna. Gehenna wasn't a trash dump.[10] It was so much worse. It was the place where children were burned and murdered. So Jesus uses Gehenna as an image for the fiery place of God's judgment (Isaiah 66:23–24; Mark 9:42–50; Revelation 20).

As a result of Ahaz's distrust and sinful actions, there were long-term consequences when God finally showed up. The Assyrians would be the first wave of foreign rulers who took over the reins of the kingdoms of Israel and Judah.

Sometimes, there are long-term consequences for disobeying or not trusting in God. The consequences we endure (whether from our own choices or the choices of others) don't negate God's love for us. Acknowledging our shortcomings and mistakes and asking God to deal with them is an opportunity for us to help make the world a better place when we allow God to act. For God to truly be present with his people, he has to set things right through both acts of mercy and justice. Are we willing to acknowledge both our successes and failings and to ask God to show up? To make our lives right? To make the world right?

How Matthew Uses Isaiah

Now, stick with me. This kind of reading that points to Isaiah's prophecy being fulfilled in Isaiah's day does not undermine what Matthew is doing.

Some people see these kinds of prophecies as having a double fulfillment. The imagery used is sometimes a mountain range. We see multiple peaks together, but we have no idea of the distance between the mountains. So Isaiah's prophecy concerns events in his day as well as the time of Jesus. For myself, I find this kind of claim less convincing. It feels very

10. Associating Gehenna with a trash dump is an unfortunate myth perpetuated by pastors and commentators. It is a significantly later tradition, possibly begun with Rabbi David Kimchi (about AD 1200), as noted by Beasley-Murray, *Jesus and the Kingdom of God*, 376n92.

subjective in terms of how do we know which prophecies are near and which are still far away.

I prefer to understand Matthew using the idea of "typology." What's typology? Many of us have taken various personality tests over the years. Past trends have included the Myers-Briggs Test, while more recently, people rave about Enneagrams. These personality tests ask general questions in an attempt to associate us with similar minded people. We aren't reduced down to these specific types, but they can help determine some of our general characteristics.

In literature, when we talk about "typology," we describe a phenomenon of general qualities or characteristics that several things may share. In stories, we may have hero-types, villain-types, the mysterious stranger-types, and so forth. In this case, Matthew is creating connections between the virgin and child in Isaiah and Mary and Jesus. By citing Isaiah, Matthew is recalling this story of the miracle of a virgin having a child that the prophet predicted. This birth was a sign of Israel's salvation and impending judgment when "God is with us."

For Matthew this miracle is "supersized." Mary isn't just a young woman who gets pregnant at the right time. Rather, she experiences a virginal *conception*—no man was involved. This miracle is a sign of God's work among his people through the ministry of Jesus. When we look at Jesus's ministry, we discover that it is similar to Isaiah's dual message of salvation and judgment.[11] Jesus preaches a message of salvation, for those who seek it, but also judgment, especially for the political and religious leaders who reject him.

Further, God does not merely show up in some general sense of his presence. Instead, God is actually present in the person of Jesus (Matthew 18:20; 25:31–46; 28:20). Matthew's Gospel also ends with a promise in the "Great Commission" that Jesus remains present with his disciples when he says, "I am with you *always*, even to the end of the age" (Matthew 28:20).[12]

This promise of Jesus's presence with his people carries into our lives today. Jesus is still present with his people. Wherever we go, we carry the presence of Jesus to others. Is the presence of Jesus making a difference in our lives or the lives of others? Do people experience Jesus's presence

---

11. One example of Jesus preaching a similar message of salvation and judgment like Isaiah is seen in Mark 4:11–12 (parallel in Matthew 13:11–17; Luke 8:10) when Jesus cites Isaiah 6:9–10 to explain his use of parables.

12. Ziesler, "Matthew and the Presence of Jesus," 55–63, 90–97.

through our lives? I am reminded of my friends who have told me, "If only Jesus would appear, then I would believe him." With these statements, I'm convicted because I clearly haven't been doing a very good job being the presence of Jesus to others.

Just as Isaiah spoke of a sign showing God was present with his people in times of trouble during the days of Ahaz, so Matthew speaks of a new, even more amazing sign of God's presence with his people through Jesus becoming a human baby. Do we expect God to show up during our times of trouble? Do we have an expectant hope that God will act, or has our trust been reduced to wishful thinking?

The difference between hope and wishful thinking is that hope builds upon looking at God's track record. We trust God because we've seen him act in the past—either in our own lives or the lives of others. Wishful thinking is disconnected from reality and ignores the past. The Bible tells these stories to remind us of how God has acted in the past so that we can trust him to act in similar ways in the present and future.

Elsewhere in the Bible, God's presence is described when Christians are called the body of Christ (1 Corinthians 12:12–31; Ephesians 4:1–16). In this world, we are called to be the hands and feet of Jesus. When people cry, do they feel Jesus when we hug them? When people are in need, do our hands look like Jesus is providing for them? When we see injustice, are the feet of Jesus carrying us swiftly to help? As the church, how are we carrying on the legacy of Immanuel, God with us? Christmas is a chance for us to celebrate, remember, and be challenged by the day God came to dwell with people.

Reflection Questions

1. How do babies change their parents' lives? Do you know anyone who had a surprise pregnancy? Alternatively, recall a movie or television show where babies are prominent. How do you think the baby Jesus changed the lives of his parents?

2. How does God use babies and childbirth to bring hope to Ahaz as well as to Joseph and Mary? How can babies bring hope today? How can we help those who do not find hope in the birth of a child or have lost a child?

3. How does God help Ahaz with the problems he faces? What consequences does Ahaz face for his sinful actions? Are we willing to acknowledge both our successes and failings and to ask God to show up and make things right?

4. How does Matthew 1:22–23 build upon the story of Ahaz and "supersize" the miracle of the virgin birth? Is there an area where you would like to see an extra measure of God's power to act?

5. God kept his promises—both to save and to hold people accountable—in both Isaiah's day and Jesus's day. What promises does God make to his people today?

6. Let's think about God's presence. How was God present with the people of Israel during Isaiah's day? How was God with his people in the life of Jesus?

7. How is God with his people today? Where do you need God to show up in your life?

8. How can the church convey God's presence in the world? Do people sense the presence of Jesus in your life? What can you do to help others feel God's presence?

Activity: Breath Prayers

In this chapter we learned how the Christmas story reminds us of God being present with his people. So, how can we feel God's presence today? One way that we can practice the presence of God is through our prayer life. One prayer technique is called a breath prayer. A breath prayer focuses prayers on our breathing. So, try breathing in while praying "more of you" as your lungs fill with air. Then exhale while praying "less of me." Alternatively, in the Christmas season, inhale and pray "Immanuel," then exhale and pray "God with us." The aim is to make prayer as natural as breathing. Periodically through your day, take a moment to just take a deep breath and pray.

7

Ruining the Inn—Rediscovering the Guest Room

Christians have been doing Christmas shows for about 800 years. Saint Francis of Assisi is credited with organizing the first live manger scene in 1223 at the Italian town of Greccio.[1]

In my twenties, I lived in southern California. Each Christmas, one of the Christmas season's biggest events happened at a church just down the road from Disneyland called the Crystal Cathedral.

Growing up in a small, rural town in northern California, I would never have imagined the sensory spectacle of going to church and seeing real people dressed like angels and zipping on wires over my head. Nor could I fathom being inside a church watching Mary riding a real donkey, shepherds sitting among real sheep, or magi leading real camels excreting the occasional real poop.

A lot went into the Crystal Cathedral's show, and the narrator stressed the pageant's historical authenticity. So, sprinkled throughout the show would be historical "facts." For example, we were told that Jesus was really

1. Smith, "Christmas," 3:659.

born in a cave, not a stable, because caves were used to house animals in the first century. In fact, identifying Jesus's birthplace as a cave isn't new. We've already read about the Infancy Gospel of James portraying Jesus's birth in a cave. Justin Martyr also argued that Jesus was born in a cave because his family couldn't find lodging in the village.[2]

Christmas can be a busy time of year for small petting zoos, which end up renting out their animals to churches to help add another layer of "authenticity" to their shows. However, I've got some sad news for all those Christmas programs. Except for the shepherds' sheep, no animals are mentioned in the original Christmas stories. Certainly, this would disappoint the donkey that was the main character in the Christmas cartoon movie, *The Star*. There is no donkey found in any of our four Gospels' stories, but the donkey is added in the Infancy Gospel of James.

Including a donkey is understandable. The journey from Nazareth to Bethlehem was a considerable distance of 85 miles. This would have taken up to a week to traverse. It certainly would have been nice to have an animal for this kind of journey. But as a poor Jewish family, it is unlikely that Mary and Joseph could have afforded such an animal.

No Room in the Inn Because There Was No Inn

While it may not be very shocking to have a beloved animal missing from the original story, it may come as a surprise that there also was no inn (and hence no innkeeper) in this story.

The innkeeper and inn's entire presence is based on translating the Greek word *katalyma* (pronounced kat-al-oo-mah[3]) as "inn." Hence, Luke 2:7 reads, "She wrapped him in bands of cloth, and laid him in a manger, because there was no place for them in the *inn*." It turns out that while the word can mean "inn," it can also be translated as "guest room." So, newer translations of Luke 2:7 read, "Because there was no *guest room* available for them" (NIV).

So what is the best translation of the *katalyma*? Should it be "inn" as traditionally thought or "guest room"? In favor of "guest room," we discover that Luke uses this same word at the end of the Gospel to describe

2. Justin Martyr, *Dialogue with Trypho* 78 (AD 155–65), Infancy Gospel of James (late second century), Origen, *Against Celsus* 1.51 (AD 185–254), and Eusebius, *De Vita Constantini* 3.43; *De laudibus Constantini* 9 (fourth century).

3. "A" as in father and "y" as in book.

the location of the Last Supper (Luke 22:11). Further, Luke uses a different word for "inn," *pandocheion* (pronounced pan-dokk-i-on[4]), in the parable of the Good Samaritan to describe where the hurt man is left (Luke 10:34). So, if Luke had meant "inn" in the birth stories, he would have used "inn" (*pandocheion*) instead of "guest room" (*katalyma*).[5]

Now let's consider these translations using our imaginations. We've been taught this picture of a tired and desperate Joseph and Mary going from inn to inn or house to house, knocking on doors (preferably in the dark, and in the rain), but unable to find any room to stay. Finally, they come across a kindly innkeeper, who doesn't have any rooms due to the Roman census. However, he takes pity on the young couple and escorts them to his stable. They make do with these circumstances, and in the middle of the night, surrounded by barnyard animals, Jesus is born.

This scene is easy for us to imagine. We tend to think of what it would be like to visit some city when there was a major event occurring, like traveling home for Thanksgiving, attending the Olympic Games, or being at San Diego's Comic-Con. We wouldn't be surprised if we hadn't booked our hotel in advance and we couldn't find a room.

But now, let's shift our imaginations a bit to consider the possibility of a "guest room."[6] Imagine that it's Christmas time (appropriate, right?), and you are going to visit some relatives. In most cases, you probably would stay with your family, possibly in your old room or a guest room (or a room where the kids have been kicked out). You probably wouldn't be trying to book a hotel room. I understand that you may immediately think of the house being too small for everyone to stay or some conflict has arisen so that people chose not to stay together. But I would also imagine that, given a choice, most of us would stay with our families when visiting from out of town. It would only be from extenuating circumstances that we wouldn't stay with them.

So, which of our imagined scenarios makes the most sense of the biblical story? We have to remember that Luke tells us that Mary and Joseph return to Bethlehem for the Roman census because this is where Joseph's

---

4. "A" as in f*a*ther, "o" as in n*o*t, "ch" as in lo*ch*, and "ei" as in *ei*ght.

5. In addition, the verbal form of the word, *katalyō*, which often means "to loose, destroy," also means "to find lodging" or "be a guest" as in Luke 9:12 and 19:7. Green, *Luke*, 128–29.

6. Bailey, "Manger and the Inn," 33–44. Bailey, *Jesus through Middle Eastern Eyes*, 32–33.

family is from (Luke 2:1–4). That means that there would likely be relatives in town who had homes with guest rooms.

It is also helpful to know that there were not many inns or hotels in the ancient world. Further, because Bethlehem was a small town of about one thousand people, the presence of an inn would be even less likely. Travelers often relied upon a network of hospitality and only stayed at inns, which had bad reputations, as a last resort. These inns are a far cry from modern-day Hiltons or Embassy Suites. If you've ever seen the musical *Les Misérables,* then you might imagine the corrupt innkeeper and his wife. They are introduced into the story while singing about being the "master of the house" while stealing from their customers.

So, in reconstructing this story using literary evidence, our imaginations guided by practical experience, and historical knowledge, it makes better sense that Mary and Joseph were not attempting to stay in some "inn." Instead, they were trying to stay with Joseph's extended family. But due to the census, the home was full, and there was no space in the "guest room."

Away in the Manger

So, if there was no room for Mary and Joseph in the usual "guest room," then where did they stay, and where was this "manger"? To help us understand this better, we need to know a little bit more about where people kept their animals.

Israelite shepherds kept their animals in a walled enclosure or a cave with a stone fence built across the opening to protect the animals.[7] Because of the many caves in the Bethlehem area, it is possible that shepherds in this region used the caves. So, the early traditions of Jesus being born in a cave are plausible.

However, we also know that during this period, Israelites would bring their animals into their homes during the night. In a typical home, the front of the house would be the space where the animals were gathered for the night. In a region that became rather cool at night, bringing the animals inside the house added warmth as well as assured their protection. In this animals' space would be the manger for their food. Further into the house,

---

7. Sheep were either kept in a simple walled enclosure (Numbers 32:16; John 10:1) or caves (1 Samuel 24:3). Vancil, "Sheep, Shepherd," 5:1187.

the family would sleep in a living area that was often elevated. The back or roof of the house would be the location of the "guest room."[8]

So, it is likely that when Mary and Joseph arrived in Bethlehem, the house was so full that there was no room for them in the main sleeping space or the guest room, so they had to sleep with the animals. When baby Jesus was born, he was placed in the manger. He was wrapped in swaddling clothes, which were not signs of poverty, but demonstrated Mary's maternal care. For example, Ezekiel 16:4 speaks of an infant's proper care, including cutting the umbilical cord, washing, rubbing with salt, and wrapping in cloth.[9]

Why Was There No Room?

Now Luke does not tell us the reason why there was no room for them in the guest room, so we must speculate. Some people read this story in a positive light. The family, under the constraints of a full house, did the best they could and gave Jesus a place in the manger. Others see Jesus's placement in the manger as a symbolic contrast to Isaiah 1:3, which says, "The ox knows its master, the donkey its owner's manger, but Israel does not know, my people do not understand."[10] According to Isaiah, Israel lacked understanding, but Luke teaches that the Messiah's birth brings new insight to God's people.

However, it is more likely that the family is ashamed of Mary and Joseph because Mary became pregnant during her betrothal. If Joseph has stuck to his claims that he is not Jesus's father, then Jesus would be seen as an illegitimate child, bringing further shame upon the family (Deuteronomy 22:20, 25–27).[11]

We find hints of this shame in the Gospel accounts. Matthew's Gospel addresses Joseph's concerns about the child's legitimacy with the angel

---

8. This is a standard description of a first-century Jewish home found in commentaries. For example, Nolland, *Luke*, 1:105–6. This is different from the homes of Greco-Roman urban dwellers or ancient Israelite homes.

9. The Jewish writing, Wisdom of Solomon 7:4–5 also includes a royal connection with swaddling clothes: "I was nursed with care in swaddling clothes. For no king has had a different beginning of existence; there is for all one entrance into life, and one way out."

10. Giblin, "Reflections on the Sign of the Manger," 87–101.

11. However, Brown (*Birth of the Messiah*, 535–42) does not read any signs of illegitimacy in the Gospel texts.

making statements like "the child conceived in her is from the Holy Spirit" (Matthew 1:20). We are told that Joseph was "unwilling to expose her to public disgrace," so he "planned to dismiss her quietly" (Matthew 1:19). In Luke's Gospel, Jesus reminds his parents that God, not Joseph, is his Father (Luke 1:48–49). These passages show that paternal questions surrounded Jesus's birth. In John 8:41, Jesus's opponents say, "We are not illegitimate children," which may be hinting that Jesus's enemies were claiming that he was illegitimate.

At least from the second century, charges of Jesus's illegitimacy were filed by various opponents of Christianity. For example, around AD 177–180 Celsus wrote,

> It was Jesus himself who fabricated the story that he had been born of a virgin. In fact, however, his mother was a poor country woman who earned her living by spinning. She had been driven out by her carpenter-husband when she was convicted of adultery with a soldier named Panthera.[12]

If the family thought that Joseph impregnated Mary, then the shame of this pregnancy could be undone by their marriage (Deuteronomy 22:29). If people thought Jesus was illegitimate, then the best that could be hoped for was that Joseph would adopt him. In today's culture, we sometimes hold similar stigmas of shame on young women who get pregnant before marriage. Growing up, I had several friends who could share the story of "mom and dad got married, and three months later I was born."

So, it is quite possible that Joseph's family was ashamed of Mary and Joseph. Instead of giving the young, pregnant woman a space in the guest room, they forced her to sleep and give birth among the animals.

Lessons of Rejection

What lessons can we learn from this? When we look at the stories of Mary and Joseph, we can ask how well do churches respond to teenage pregnancies? What kind of support network do we provide for young mothers? Are we teaching our young men to take responsibility for their actions? (After

12. Cited by Origen, *Against Celsus*, 1.28.32.69. See also *Jerusalem Talmud Aboda Zara* 40d, *Sabbath* 14d. Others claimed the father was Ben Stada (*Babylonian Talmud Sabbath* 104b, *Sanhedrin* 67a). Tertullian (*De Spectaculis* 30.6; about AD 197) refuted charges that Jesus was a son of a prostitute. See the discussion in Brown, *Birth of the Messiah*, 534–37.

all, two people are involved in pregnancies, but how often do we just shame women?) Do we provide a place of dignity and respect, or do we show condemnation and shame? Are there services as simple as babysitting, providing meals, or giving educational support to help young parents?

Even as a child, Jesus understood what it meant to be rejected. He understood what it meant to be defined by the choices his parents made. Jesus was looked down on because of his parents. His own family rejected him, even at his birth.

This rejection is recapitulated when his hometown of Nazareth rejected and tried to kill him as an adult in Luke 4:16–30. It is described when Jesus declares that allegiance to him results in dividing families (Luke 12:49–53). Finally, this rejection anticipates when the leaders of Jesus's own people reject him so that he is crucified on a Roman cross (Luke 23:13–25).

Have we experienced rejection because of our families? Kids who change schools, cities, or even countries can experience rejection because of their parents' choices. I remember how hard it was to make friends at my new school when my parents moved when I was a kid. What about children who live difficult lives because of growing up with single parents or divorced parents? Jesus understands what it is like to face challenges because of choices made by others outside of our control.

A New Guestroom

As we've noted already, Luke only mentions the "guest room" twice in his Gospel. Here at the beginning (Luke 2:7), and then at the end during the Last Supper (Luke 22:11). Luke portrays the Last Supper as a Passover meal (Luke 22:7–38). The Passover was typically a meal where families would gather together once a year to remember the exodus story (Exodus 12–13; Leviticus 23). Families, who were able, would travel to Jerusalem to participate in the Passover festival. They would eat lamb and unleavened bread together. They would tell stories of God's great act of deliverance of the Israelites from the oppression of Egypt.[13] This beautiful meal of remembrance is still practiced by Jewish families today.

What is surprising about Jesus's Last Supper is that his family is absent from the meal. Instead, he instructs two of his disciples, Peter and John, to

---

13. On the history and background of Passover as it has developed from the Old Testament to the New Testament to current times, see Bokser, "Unleavened Bread and Passover, Feasts of," 6:755–65.

follow a mysterious stranger who will provide a place for them to prepare the meal. During the meal, Jesus shares unleavened bread and wine with his disciples. He tells them about God's new plans of salvation through his upcoming death on the cross. Jesus appears to have made a new family of his disciples, where they have gathered together to remember God's past acts of salvation and promises of new days of redemption.

Luke sets up a contrast between these "guest rooms." At the beginning of his Gospel, Jesus's extended family rejects him at his birth by offering no space in the guest room. At the end of his Gospel, Jesus has created a new family and offers a space for anyone to join him in the guest room, including his betrayer Judas.

One of the powerful messages of Christmas is that Jesus came to this earth to create a new family. If you have good relationships with your family, congratulations! Your healthy relationships can help others to have healthy family relationships. However, Jesus also wants to remind us that his family is bigger than being blood relatives. For anyone without a positive relationship with their fathers, mothers, siblings, or extended family, Jesus comes to this earth to help form a new family. If you have family problems at Christmas, remember the family problems Jesus had.

While our earthly parents might disappoint or reject us, God never will. While our siblings may let us down, Jesus, as our brother, never does. The message of Christmas is that we belong. We are part of a new community, a family that loves us. Being part of this family gives us a new identity.

While we are part of a new family, it isn't perfect. Just like we can get hurt by our earthly families, so our spiritual family can hurt us. Also, we can hurt others in our family. Yet, however much we may hurt each other, we are still family. At the same time, being part of God's family does not excuse bad behavior. Sometimes we have to set up healthy boundaries within our church families, especially when it comes to protecting the young and vulnerable.

As we think about Christmas, are we going to treat our spiritual family like Jesus's earthly family treated him on that first Christmas? Will we reject others? Will we shame them? Or will we treat others like Jesus did on that final Passover? Will we invite anyone to our table? Will we show hospitality to people who don't look like us or act like us? Will we show love to others for the simple reason that we're family?

Reflection Questions

1. If you could play any character in the Christmas story, who would it be and why? If you've ever played a Christmas character, recall that story.

2. Whom do you picture surrounding Jesus during his birth? Who would have delivered the baby? What kind of emotions would Mary and Joseph feel? Besides swaddling clothes, what kind of things would be done to take care of the newborn?

3. Where do you imagine Jesus was born? Is it easier to imagine Jesus being born in an inn or a guest room? Does the location make any different?

4. Jesus's family lived in an honor-shame culture. Have you ever thought about the shame that Mary and Joseph may have felt about Mary's pregnancy before they were married? Have you thought about Jesus growing up with the shame of being considered an illegitimate child? Why do you think that these charges of illegitimacy were leveled against Jesus even into the second century? Are there things that you are ashamed about that you could hand over to God?

5. Jesus understands what it is like to face challenges because of others' choices made outside of our control. Have you ever faced difficulties in life because of your parents' decisions?

6. What are ways that we can support young families? How do we help children feel cared for and valued?

7. Reflect upon the two guestrooms in Luke's Gospel. While Jesus's family rejected him and kept him out of the guest room, Jesus makes room for his new family in the guest room at the Lord's Supper. How do we make room for others as part of God's family?

8. The two guestrooms also remind us of the importance of hospitality. How can we practice hospitality?

Activity: Hospitality

As we explored the significance of the two guestrooms, we learned the importance of hospitality in ancient Israel. The premiere examples of good hosts versus bad hosts come from Genesis 18. Abram and Sarah are good hosts who entertain angels. The people of Sodom are bad hosts because they try to abuse these angels. When we practice godly hospitality, we bring God's presence and blessings to ourselves and others. Look for a way to show hospitality to someone this week. With whom could you share a meal or a coffee? Is there a neighbor that you could reach out to? How can we practice hospitality this Christmas season?

8

Ruining the Silent Night—
Rediscovering Real Peace

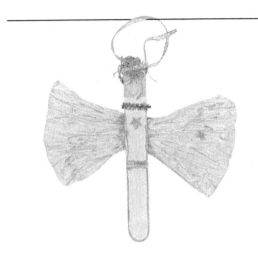

During college, I took a sculpting class. One of my favorite assignments was to make a sculpture by bending wire. Using wire felt like drawing with a three-dimensional pencil. Before this, I had always stuck to the two-dimensional space of a piece of paper or canvas. It felt liberating to be able to work in three dimensions, and I began to bend a whole array of wire sculptures for family and friends.

One of my favorite creations was a small wire sculpture of three angels flying around baby Jesus lying in his manger. My dad, being his usual supportive self, saw my sculpture and asked me to transform my tiny angels circling Jesus into ten-foot giants that we would string with Christmas lights and hang in the oak trees of our front yard during Christmas time.

During the year, you could come over to my parents' house and you would see a strange tangle of wire in the corner of our garage. You might wonder why my parents would let such an ugly, tangled mess take up so much precious garage space. But if you came by my parents' house during the Christmas season, you would be captivated by these glowing angels that seemed to defy gravity as they circled in the sky around a manger.

Shepherds and Sheep

We learn about the angels appearing to the shepherds from Luke 2:8–20, while Matthew 2:1–12 tells us a different story of the magi being led by a star. There are various explanations about who these shepherds were and why God would invite them to the first Christmas celebration.[1]

One popular theory is that these shepherds were tending the vast flocks of the sheep necessary for the temple sacrifices (*Mishnah Sheqalim* 7:4).[2] From this perspective, we get a bit of foreshadowing of Jesus's impending sacrifice on the cross. These shepherds, whose job was to prepare and keep safe the sheep that were sacrificed for the people, are called to bear witness to the birth of the "lamb" of God who would take away the sins of the world (John 1:29).

Another popular view points out that shepherds did not always have the best reputation in the ancient world. Because of their wandering nature, shepherds had a reputation for being untrustworthy. (This may remind us of the unfair stereotypes that we place upon people like immigrants or when the Romani people are called "gypsies.") Thus, the Jewish author Philo writes, "Such occupations are accounted inglorious and mean" (*Agriculture* 61). Another Jewish rabbi, Abba Gurion quips, "Their trade is the trade of thieves" (*Mishnah Qiddushin* 4.14).

We also see this ancient prejudice against shepherds in the Old Testament stories of the wanderings of Abraham, Isaac, and Jacob. As shepherds, they were never fully accepted by the people of the land and were often treated with mistrust (Genesis 21:22–34). Even when the Israelites settled in Egypt, they were separated to the land of Goshen due to the ill repute of shepherds (Genesis 45:20; 46:28–34).

---

1. On shepherds and sheep in the Old Testament and New Testament, see Vancil, "Sheep, Shepherd," 5:1187–91.

2. Plummer, *Luke*, 54.

For Christians, this negative view of shepherds can be challenging to reconcile with images of Jesus being our "good shepherd" who is willing to lay down his life for his sheep (John 10:11, 14) or positive images of God as our shepherd (Psalm 23:1; Genesis 48:15). Major heroes like Abel, Abraham, Isaac, Jacob, and Moses were shepherds (Genesis 4:2–4; 30:37–43; Exodus 3:1–2). Further, the presence of the shepherds fits the pastoral setting of Bethlehem, the hometown of the former shepherd, King David (1 Samuel 16:11; 17:15; Psalm 77).

So, we have to be careful not to fall into the trap of flatly stereotyping people groups. In fact, another possibility sees these shepherds positively. It is because God so closely identifies himself as a shepherd of his people (Psalm 23:1; Genesis 48:15) that God chose to reveal the birth of his Son to shepherds.

Even if we hesitate to go so far as to see these shepherds as characters of ill repute, we can at least note that the shepherds would have been ordinary, poor folk. Luke creates a contrast between Jesus being revealed to these lowly shepherds instead of the elite rulers of Emperor Augustus and Governor Quirinius.[3] The invitation to the shepherds is an invitation to the outsider, the weirdo, and the least likely of people to bear witness to the miracle of Jesus.

As we reflect on this story, we may ask ourselves how does Jesus meet us in our own insecurities? Do we ever feel like we don't really belong? How much energy do we expend trying to fit in? Think about the clothes we wear, the shows we watch, the things we read, the food we eat, and the teams we root for. Could the story of the shepherds help relieve our stress from needing to fit in, knowing that God is the one who wishes to include us? How do churches welcome outsiders, immigrants, the poor, or the lonely? How do we make churches safe places for everyone to belong? Can our church communities be opportunities for insiders and outsiders to gather around the manger?

While Matthew describes the three gifts of the magi, Luke tells us about a different sort of treasure. In response to the visit of the shepherds, Luke 2:19 tells us that Mary "treasured all these words and pondered them in her heart." The angels' revelation about Jesus's identity as well as the visit from these unlikely visitors was something of value to Mary. Do we value the chance for people from all walks of life to gather around Jesus? Do we treasure the presence of others as valuable?

3. Horsley, *Liberation of Christmas*, 100–106.

Rome Rocks! Rocking Rome

After explaining in his first chapter how Jesus is coming to fulfill the hopes and dreams of Israel as their Messiah, Luke broadens the story beyond a backwater nation to set the scene in terms of the global concerns of the Roman Empire. In those days, Rome was in charge. Israel was simply a territory at the fringe of the empire.

It is not an accident that Augustus is named (Luke 2:2). He is the founding emperor of the Roman Empire. By mentioning Augustus, Luke contrasts Jesus as Messiah with the Roman emperor.[4] Jesus's miraculous birth would be compared with Augustus's birth. The Roman historian Suetonius (*Divus Augustus* 94.4) claimed that Augustus was the son of the god, Apollo. He tells the story of Augustus being divinely conceived. While in the form of a serpent, Apollo miraculously impregnated Augustus's mother, Atia. In contrast to the vulgarity of Suetonius, Luke claims that Mary became pregnant by the Holy Spirit without any divine intercourse.

Further, many of the titles for the Roman emperor, including "Lord" and "Son of God," were used for Jesus. These titles would have created a comparison between Jesus and the emperor. Understanding the emperor as "Lord" (Greek, *kyrios*) was so important that in a period slightly later than the New Testament, Christians were given a choice between declaring Jesus as Lord or Caesar as Lord (Martyrdom of Polycarp 8–10).[5] Those who would not declare Caesar as their Lord were killed. Declaring Jesus as Lord was a statement of allegiance or loyalty to Jesus. A declaration of Jesus's lordship indicated who you thought was in charge. A modern equivalent might be to call Jesus the president, king, or boss.

Luke's Gospel begins with the angels declaring the birth of the "Lord" (Luke 2:11), and it ends with Jesus's disciples proclaiming, "The Lord has risen" (Luke 24:34). With this title Luke is claiming that Jesus is in charge. Death on a Roman cross could not defeat him.

In today's world, loyalty is still prized. Our credit card companies and businesses have "loyalty" programs. Our loyalty is rewarded with certain benefits. In the ancient world, loyalty was also important. One of the key terms for describing this loyalty was the Greek word *pistis*, which our

4. Brown, *Birth of the Messiah*, 415. For a comparison between Jesus and Caesar, see Horsley, *Liberation of Christmas*, 25–33.

5. See Witherington and Yamazaki-Ransom, "Lord," 526–35. "Lord" was also used as a title of respect (e.g., Matthew 8:2) as well as a translation for Yahweh (e.g., Matthew 3:3).

Bibles often translate as "faith." While Rome expected "faith" or "loyalty" to the emperor, Luke's Gospel asks people to demonstrate their "faith" or "loyalty" to Jesus.[6]

Christianity is not just about knowing the right ideas or holding to the right beliefs. Christianity involves acting upon these beliefs. The mixture of action and belief is described well with the term "loyalty." How do we show loyalty to Jesus today? What are the benefits we receive because of this loyalty?

Let's turn to the title, "Son of God."[7] When Julius Caesar died, there was a comet that shot across the sky. Augustus proclaimed that this comet was Julius's soul ascending to heaven to take his place as a god. Claiming that Julius was a god, Augustus was the first Roman emperor to be granted the title "Son of God" to remind his subjects of his special connection to the gods.

As "Son of God," Augustus enjoyed divine privileges and could ask for divine favors. As "Son of God," honors, sacrifices, and temples were erected to pay tribute to him. This was not some obscure title that only a few people knew. The title "Son of God" was inscribed on many Roman coins, including the silver denarii (Mark 12:16).

When Mary is told that her child will be called the "Son of God" (Luke 1:35), Luke's audience would immediately contrast Jesus with the most famous "Son of God" in the Roman Empire, the emperor. By specifically naming Emperor Augustus (Luke 2:1) just before Jesus's birth, Luke is alerting his audience that they should be contrasting these two "Sons of Gods."

These competing claims of divine sonship come out most forcibly at the end of Jesus's ministry when he is asked about paying taxes to Caesar (Mark 12:13–17; Matthew 22:15–22; Luke 20:20–26). In response, Jesus asks for a silver denarius and points out the Roman coin's inscription and image. The inscription and image violated two of the Ten Commandments. The inscription that proclaimed Caesar as "Son of God" violated the command against worshiping other gods (Exodus 20:3). Caesar's image on the coin would violate the related command to not make idols (Exodus 20:4). Jesus's proclamation of "give to Caesar the things of Caesar" is not a

---

6. Bates, *Gospel Allegiance*; McKnight, *King Jesus Gospel*.

7. Winn, "Son of God," 886–94. In the Bible, "son of God" can also refer to the Davidic king (Psalm 2:7; 2 Samuel 7:13–14), Adam (Luke 3:38), as well as divine beings like angels (Genesis 6:2; Job 1:6; Daniel 3:25).

statement about paying taxes. Instead, Jesus is boldly telling people to give back to Caesar his idolatrous coins.

In contrast, Jesus says "to give to God the things of God." What are the "things" that Jesus is talking about? Is this a statement to pay the church a tithe, that is, 10 percent of your income? Not quite. We need a little backstory in order to understand this statement. In fact, we have to go all the way back to the very beginning of the Bible. When God created people in Genesis 1, we discover that "God created humankind in his image, in the image of God he created them" (Genesis 1:27). Thus, all people bear the image of God.

The image of Caesar indicated the empire's ownership of the coin. Likewise, people bearing the image of God indicate God's ownership of people. Just as the emperor used his image to mark his ownership of his coin, so Jesus knew that God used his image to mark people to show God's ownership of humanity. By saying "give to Caesar the things of Caesar" Jesus challenges his audience to give back to Caesar his idolatrous money. By expecting people "to give to God the things of God," he challenges them to give to God their whole selves.

Just as Jesus didn't divide people or their money into sacred and secular parts, we should not compartmentalize our resources or our personhood. We can ask ourselves if we are people who are giving ourselves wholly to God? What are we doing with our resources? Do we treat other people as God's prized possessions? If we take seriously God's ownership of people, then our entire worldview is changed.

Things like slavery and human trafficking are wrong because the Bible opens with a story that tells us that people shouldn't own other people because the true owner of each person is our creator, God. People don't have the right to own other people. People are not our property. They are God's possessions. Do we treat others as God's precious possessions? Do we see how special others truly are? The primary reason that we should love our neighbor (Leviticus 19:18) is because they have been made in the image of God. When we look at ourselves in the mirror, or when we look at other people, whose face do we see? Do we just see our own face? Or do we catch a glimpse of God's face looking back at us?

Really Good News

Three related terms—"gospel," "peace," and "Savior"—were used by both the emperor and Jesus. In modern times, the term "gospel" sounds very "Christian." However, in the ancient world, the word "gospel" (Greek, *euangelion*), which means "good news," was not a term exclusively used by Christians.[8]

In fact, it was often connected to the proclamation of benevolent acts of the Roman emperor.[9] It was considered "good news" when a famine or plague ended. It was "good news" when the emperor defeated his enemies. And in one famous inscription from Priene in Asia Minor (about 9 BC), the birth of Emperor Augustus was proclaimed as "good news." Did you catch that? The birth of the first Roman emperor was called the "gospel" or "good news" (*euangelion*).

One of the things that Augustus was most famous for was bringing "peace" to the Roman Empire. This peace was called the "Roman Peace" (Latin, *pax Romana*). After Julius Caesar was assassinated, the empire was plunged into civil war. After years of fighting bloody battles, Augustus, through the might of his armies defeated Marc Anthony. With this victory, Augustus became the uncontested ruler of the Roman Empire in 31 BC. The resulting "peace" was considered "gospel" or "good news" (*euangelion*).

By bringing peace, Augustus was understood to be the "Savior" of the Roman Empire. The Roman army with its legions was famous for keeping the peace, and Roman roads allowed the army to move quickly across the empire to put down revolts. The Jewish people would feel the full might of Roman peacekeeping when the Roman army destroyed Jerusalem and the temple in AD 70.

In contrast to this kind of bloody peace, the angels announce a "gospel" or "good news" (*euangelion*) that Jesus would be a different kind of "Savior" who would bring God's "peace" on earth (Luke 2:14). Bringing peace was a fulfillment of Old Testament expectations including an expectation of a "Prince of Peace" (Isaiah 9:5–6), a harvest of peace (Zechariah 8:12), and the abundance of peace (Psalm 72:7). Jesus came to fulfill the "good news"

---

8. The Greek word for Gospel is *euangelion*, which is a combination of two words: *eu* ("good") and *angelia* ("message"). Schenck, "Gospel: Good News," 342–45. For Jewish backgrounds, "good news" may be associated with proclaiming the message of God's reign, salvation, and peace (Isaiah 52:7).

9. Philo, *Legum allegoriae* 231; Josephus, *Jewish War* 2.618.

expectations as God's "anointed one," who came to proclaim the year of the Lord's favor to the oppressed (Isaiah 61:1–2; Luke 4:18–19).

Jesus is a "Savior" and brings "peace," not by using the sword, but by dying at the hands of those wielding the "sword" of a Roman cross. Jesus goes on to defeat his Roman death by God's resurrection power. So that when Jesus rises from the dead, he is able to proclaim "peace" to his disciples (Luke 24:36; see also John 20:21). That's "good news."

Peace Out!

Jesus's peace was not simply the cessation of war or conflict (1 Samuel 7:14) but encapsulated the Jewish concept of *shalom* or holistic peace. The Hebrew word *shalom* encapsulates a life of general well-being as expressed in this blessing found in Numbers 6:24–26:

> The LORD bless you and keep you;
> the LORD make his face to shine upon you, and be gracious to you;
> the LORD lift up his countenance upon you, and give you "peace"
> (*shalom*).

Because this peace is experienced when one's life is aligned with the will of God, we should ask ourselves what we are doing to align our lives with God's will. Romans 12:2 says, "Do not conform any longer to the pattern of this world, but be transformed by the renewing of your mind. Then you will be able to test and approve what God's will is—his good, pleasing and perfect will." Following Jesus involves having a different mindset. Our thoughts are to be like the thoughts of God. When we think like God, we can find peace. But to think like God, we need brain surgery. We need to ask our divine doctor to realign our misfiring neural pathways to conform with God's will.

Where do we need peace in our lives today? What things are stressing us out? What are our fears? Are we depressed? How are we insecure? What things keep us up at night? Are we having trouble in our relationships with friends or family? How's our job, home life, or school? Are we just looking for our conflicts to end, or can we seek something deeper and more meaningful?

Jesus came to bring true peace to his followers. God doesn't promise to take away our problems. However, God does promise to help us deal with our problems because God is bigger than any of our problems. What sort of symbols or reminders do you have in your life to remind you of God's peace?

In our family, we named our youngest son "Pax," which is the Latin word for "peace," to remind us of God's promise of peace.

Not only does the Christmas story remind us that Jesus came to this world to bring peace to our lives, but it also reminds us that this peace is for the whole world. And as followers of Jesus, we should be agents of peace in this world. Jesus says, "Blessed are the peacemakers, for they will be called sons of God" (Matthew 5:9). Jesus showed others that he was God's Son through his actions and words. Being peacemakers is one way that followers of Jesus can show others that we're also God's children.

What's sad to me is to see how often Christians get caught up with divisive social, political, and religious issues. When did we allow ourselves to become weapons of division? Are there ways to seek things like truth and justice without sacrificing those we disagree with along the way? Are Christians more concerned about holding onto power or influence than being models of what it means to lay down our lives and rights for others? Can we find peace knowing that by doing the right thing, we are pleasing God?

When Jesus was born over two thousand years ago, the angels announced that he would bring God's peace to the world. Christmas is a chance for us to pause in the busy pursuits of our lives and to evaluate how deeply God's peace has penetrated our world.

It's become cliché to wish for "world peace" partly because we know that we can't change the whole world with mere sentiment or wishful thinking. However, the whole world is made up of individuals. If we truly want to change the world and bring peace, then we need to begin with the one person whose life we have control over—ourselves.

What if we ask God to change our hearts to bring a holistic *shalom* to our life? What if we let the angels' promise of peace begin to come true in our life? Maybe we do have the power to bring the world closer to world peace, not by force or the coercion of others, but rather by our own personal submission to Jesus, the Prince of Peace.

Reflection Questions

1. Does the Christmas season bring stress and anxiety into your life, or does it bring peace?

2. When was the last time that you felt at peace? Where do we need peace in our lives and the world today? What things are stressing us out? What are our fears? How are we insecure? How do we align ourselves

with God's will so that we can experience *shalom* peace? How can we bring God's peace into the lives of others?

3. What do you imagine the shepherds to look like, smell like, and act like? Can you imagine taking care of the sheep at night? Would you be cold? Could you see anything? Would there be a fire? What would you talk about with your other shepherds?

4. Why do you think God revealed the birth of Jesus to ordinary people like the shepherds? How worthy do you think they felt seeing baby Jesus? Do we ever feel like we don't really belong? How do we welcome outsiders, immigrants, the poor, or the lonely?

5. In what ways does Luke contrast Jesus with Emperor Augustus? How is Jesus similar to and different from those in charge of our world today? What does Jesus's example teach us about leadership?

6. What is loyalty? Why is loyalty important? What things tend to demand our loyalty? What would happen if we began to think of "faith" as "loyalty" to Jesus? How can we show loyalty to Jesus in our daily life?

7. What do we learn about taxes and tithing from Jesus's teaching about the silver denarius? What would it mean for us to give God our whole selves?

8. Has anyone ever borrowed something from you and broken it or lost it? How did that make you feel? Jesus teaches us that every person is created in the image of God, meaning they are God's property. When we look at others, do we see God's face? How should we be treating others if they are God's possessions?

Activity: Being Alone and Quiet with God

This chapter explored the ways that Jesus's birth brought peace to the world. The hustle and bustle of life, particularly during the Christmas holiday can prevent us from feeling God's peace. What would happen if we took a few moments to slow down a bit? Just as sometimes, we need to clear out some space in our closets, so we need to sometimes clear out some space in our spiritual lives. One way that we can create space is by taking some time to be alone with God. Another way is to quiet our thoughts as we attempt to listen to God. We may or may not encounter God in these moments, but they are important for making space so that God has room to show up in our lives. Can you pick a time to clear some space in your life by getting away by yourself and quieting yourself before God?

9

Ruining the Three Kings—
Rediscovering Three Fools

"Twinkle, twinkle, little star."

People are fascinated by the stars. Think of all of our star-filled expressions. "When you wish upon a star." "They were star-crossed lovers." "I'm a fan of *Star Wars*!" "No, I love *Star Trek*!" "You're a star!" "*Jesus Christ, Superstar.*"

When I think of stars at Christmas time, I can't help but remember my first Christmas tree. When I lived by myself, I had a little fake Charlie-Brown-like Christmas tree that I bought from Target on my student budget. Including ornaments and the star topper, it came out to about twenty bucks plus change. I would celebrate each year's Christmas by playing

Christmas carols and drinking hot cocoa while I unboxed my tree. Sometime after New Year's Day, I would pack my tree back up and put it away in my attic until the next year.

Speaking of Christmas trees, the Christmas tree is likely a Germanic tradition. However, its origins are debated and shrouded by myths.[1] According to one legend, St. Boniface (AD 675–754) chopped down an oak tree, which Germanic villagers were using to sacrifice humans. In its place grew a small evergreen as a symbol of the pagans' new faith and the birth of Jesus. Another tradition claims that Martin Luther (AD 1483–1546) covered a fir tree with candles explaining that the tree represented Christ as the light of the world. An alternative story tells of a woodcutter who took care of a poor, freezing child. This child ended up being the Christ-child, who gave a twig that would blossom each year.

Regardless of its origins, the Christmas tree became popular in the United States during the mid-1830s. Some trace Christmas tree traditions arriving with German immigrants in Pennsylvania in the early 1800s. According to one account, the first American Christmas tree was set up in Massachusetts in 1832 by a German abolitionist and pastor named Charles Follen. I like this tradition because each time I put up my Christmas tree I am reminded of the importance of being against slavery and racism.

Okay, now back to my star-topped tree. When I got married, one of the first things to go was my trusty Christmas tree. We upgraded to a larger, fuller, and more adult-like fake tree. (Before you judge me too harshly for my fake tree, I'll have you know that I'm allergic to Christmas trees.) Christmas still involves unpacking my tree every year and not trudging in the snow or driving to some Christmas tree lot to get a real tree.

Not only did we upgrade our tree, but we also upgraded our star to an enormous thing that I put up on our roof. During Christmas, our house is easy to spot with its giant star flashing over our roof. It certainly makes it easier to give directions to our house. While our "star of Bethlehem" doesn't mark the place of Jesus's birth, it does remind my family (and my neighbors) of that first star that marked Jesus's birth.

The star of Bethlehem is one of the signature icons of the Christmas season. Trees (and apparently houses) become complete when they are topped with the star. Of course, we read in the Christmas story that the

---

1. There are other theories about the Christmas tree's origins. In the Middle Ages, plays included a paradise tree covered with apples. Another forerunner may be the wooden Christmas pyramid from Germany. Others think the Roman custom of decorating homes with greenery persisted. See Gulevich, "Christmas Tree," 167–74.

magi were led to Jesus via a star in the sky. But who were these magi, and why would they follow a star?

Musing about the Magi

Thanks to Christmas songs like "We Three Kings of Orient Are" and various Christmas plays, Christmas art, and Christmas books that portray these men wearing crowns and dressed to impress, we have this image of the magi as royalty from the East.[2] In addition, to flesh out images of these magi, various names have been given to these anonymous visitors including Melchior, Caspar, and Balthazar.[3]

From their gifts of gold, frankincense, and myrrh, we have come to assume the number of wise men was three. However, the story doesn't actually provide a number. Others have attempted to decode these gifts. For example, according to Irenaeus (*Against the Heretics* 3.9.2), the gold reflects Jesus's kingship, frankincense his deity, and myrrh his suffering. These gifts have also been seen to connect Jesus to the Jewish high priest and temple—gold as found in the priest's clothes (Exodus 28:5–6, 11), temple incense that included frankincense (Exodus 30:34; Leviticus 2:1), and the anointing oil of myrrh used for consecration (Exodus 30:23–33).

This imagery does not come from a vacuum, and Isaiah 60 may have influenced our popular images. In this passage, we see star imagery with "Arise, shine; for your light has come" (Isaiah 60:1). The visitors are described as "kings to the brightness of your dawn" (Isaiah 60:3). Their camels (which aren't in Matthew's story) are referenced as "a multitude of camels shall cover you" (Isaiah 60:6). And their treasures are mentioned as "gold and frankincense" (Isaiah 60:6).

When we look more closely at this passage, we discover something more important than their number, their names, or their gifts' hidden symbolism. Isaiah 60 is casting a much grander vision than a few magi bringing a few gifts. Matthew sees these magi as representing all the nations of the world who have come to Israel in the last days bringing gifts.

---

2. For a critique of king images, see Powell, "Magi as Kings," 459–80. Powell notes that kingly images were established at least by the sixth century (Caesarius of Arles, *Sermo* 139; and *Cave of Treasures*), but Reformers like Luther and Calvin rejected these traditions. See also Malina, "Magi," 3:766.

3. *Excerpta Latina Barbari* 51b (AD 500).

These gifts are meant to announce God's plans for Israel and the world's restoration. So we read, "Violence shall no more be heard in your land, devastation or destruction within your borders; you shall call your walls Salvation, and your gates Praise" (Isaiah 60:18).

These magi are acting as representatives of non-Jews streaming to Israel bringing their gifts. The animosity between these two groups has been overcome. These races can be reconciled. The gathering of Jews and non-Jews around the manger reminds us that racial reconciliation is part of the heart of the gospel. There is no room for racism when people all gather to worship our common king. Jesus joins all people as his people. Matthew uses this story to include non-Jews as well as to indicate that God's promises of establishing his final kingdom were at hand.

In Matthew's day, the world had been divided between Jews and non-Jews, who were labeled as "gentiles." In other words, people were split into "us" versus "them" categories. Think about the implications of the categories of "Jews" versus "gentiles." While "Jews" defines a particular people, the term "gentiles" conflates and reduces every color of skin, every diverse language, and every different nation into *one* term.

However, with the magi's story, Matthew invites us to see the world without such divisions. While Matthew acknowledges his culture's bifurcation of people, he also challenges these categories with a vision of all people coming together to join God's kingdom. Instead of an "us" versus "them," the manger scene shows us a grander, more inclusive vision where there is simply an "us." This "us" celebrates our common humanity and celebrates differences.

Is it possible for us to capture this vision today and be agents of reconciliation? Today's society groans, longs, and demands racial justice. Christmas challenges God's people not only to take the lead in treating others with dignity and respect but also to challenge racism within and outside the church. Most importantly, Christmas calls us to be God's agents of reconciliation in the world.[4]

---

4. There is a wide range of resources available for Christians seeking to understand modern forms of racism and to be an advocate of reconciliation such as Yancey, *Beyond Racial Gridlock*; McNeil, *Roadmap to Reconciliation 2.0*; Rah, *Prophetic Lament*; McCaulley, *Reading While Black*.

The Magi Who Lost Their Magic

Can we say more to help us to identify the magi? Matthew doesn't actually describe them as kings, nor does he include details, like their camels. A more fruitful approach is to ask how Matthew's audience would have understood these magi.

What we discover is that these "wise men" weren't really kings or any kind of royalty. Rather, magi *served* kings as part of royal courts.[5] As such, some see these men functioning like royal ambassadors through their interactions with King Herod as well as their gifts presented to Jesus.

However, considering these men as ambassadors does not quite shift our understanding enough. To further shift our perspective on the magi, it might be helpful to begin by knowing that we get the word "magician" from the Greek word for "magus" (*magos*). Magi, it turns out, were part of the priestly caste, and their practices were associated with magic.

Of course, we have to be careful with this kind of word study. Countless pastors have incorrectly concluded that the Greek word for "power, ability" (*dynamis*) means "explosive power" because we get the English word "dynamite" from this word. In fact, a better image for "power" is probably the nuclear power plant that allows us to plug appliances into power outlets. We don't want to import too much of our modern ideas of magic—whether it's Harry Potter, Gandalf, or the White Witch—upon the magi.

Most likely these magi were astrologers, probably connected to the Persian religion of Zoroastrianism, who read the night sky for signs. As astrologers, they would have been keenly aware of the patterns in the sky, which they would read for heavenly signs among the stars. Understanding these magi as astrologers fits perfectly with Matthew's portrayal of these men following heavenly signs. Just as astrologers today have a mixed reputation and are even looked on with suspicion by some, these ancient astrologers also had a mixed reputation.[6]

---

5. Strabo (*Geography* 15.1.68) writes, "[They] attend the Persian kings . . . guiding them in their relationship with the gods." Xenophon (*Cyropaedia* 8.1.23–24) describes a college of the magi. Powell, "Magi as Kings," 464–65.

6. Positively, Cicero (*De divinatione* 1.23.47) describes them as wise and learned, and Pliny the Elder (*Natural Histories* 30.6.16–17) relates how Nero wished to acquire the magi's valuable knowledge. Negatively, Tacitus (*Annals* 2.27–3) denounced them, and Suetonius (*Tiberius* 36) reports that Tiberius banished all astrologers from Rome in AD 19.

In Jewish tradition, we have three significant stories that negatively portray magi.[7] First, the oldest story of magi involves Pharaoh's magicians (Exodus 7–8) who attempted to prevent Israel's exodus from Egypt.[8] These magi opposed Moses by performing counter-miracles to the initial plagues. However, the power of God proved superior to their magical arts. As Matthew echoes the exodus story, he reverses the role of the magi so that they now recognize and support God's agent of deliverance.

Second, the false prophet Balaam—the man made famous for his talking donkey—is also described as a magus by later Jewish writers.[9] Balaam was hired to curse Israel but instead prophesied about her future ruler (Numbers 22–24). Below we'll see how Balaam is important because Matthew incorporates Balaam's prophecy in Numbers 24:17 about a rising star.

Third, the most recent story of Jewish people encountering magi was found in the book of Daniel. In Babylon, Daniel became embroiled in various conflicts with the Babylonian magicians, including when they failed to interpret Nebuchadnezzar's dreams (Daniel 2:2, 10, 27; 4:7, 10; 5:11). Creating echoes with the stories from Daniel, Matthew's magi are now the ones receiving and interpreting dreams from God while the Jewish king and religious leaders remain ignorant. It would come as a surprise to Matthew's audience that these magi, who once stood opposed to the work of God, were now aligning themselves with the will of God. Some speculate that these magi learned of the Jewish Messiah from the Jewish people when they lived in Babylon.

Like Luke's lowly shepherds, Matthew's magi portray unlikely and unworthy visitors to the king of the Jews. Portraying the magi as "foolish" actually fits within Matthew's understanding of how God reveals himself. In Matthew 11:25, Jesus says, "I thank you, Father, Lord of heaven and earth, because you have hidden these things from the wise and the intelligent and have revealed them to infants." It is precisely because they are "fools" and outsiders that God reveals himself to them. These outsiders stand in contrast to the insiders of King Herod and the priests who are not granted an audience with the King of Kings.

---

7. This negative portrayal of the magi is drawn from Powell, "Magi as Wise Men," 1–20.

8. Philo, *Life of Moses*, 1.92; cf. *Babylonian Talmud Sanhedrin* 101a.

9. Philo, *Life of Moses* 1.264–305.

The Science of Stars

So what can we say about this star that led the magi to Jesus?

Growing up in the modern world, we have been taught that those stars we see when we look up in the night sky are actually giant gaseous bodies, like our sun. While our sun is about 93 million miles away, the nearest visible star, Alpha Centauri is about 25.6 trillion miles away (4.37 light-years).

The Lion King even manages to make our scientific understanding into a fart joke when the warthog, Pumbaa says, "I always thought they were balls of gas burning billions of miles away," to which his friend Timon replies, "With you, everything is gas."[10]

So, how do we match our scientific understanding of stars with the description in Matthew 2:2 and 2:9 of a star that moves by "rising" (Greek, *anatolē*), "going before" (Greek, *proagō*), and "standing" (Greek, *histēmi*)? Between examining historical records and the variety of computer simulations that can recreate accurate astrological models, there has been a proliferation of theories about this starry sign.

For many, Jupiter's movements across the sky align with Matthew's description of the star. Jupiter moves in the usual eastward direction of stars, but it also includes a period of "retrograde motion," meaning it appears to move backward across the sky. More importantly, it also "stops" before changing directions. In addition, more complex theories will link Jupiter's movements with constellations such as Pisces the fish in 7 or 6 BC, Aries the ram in 6 BC, or Leo the lion in 2 BC.

Using science to help us understand the Christmas star is not a new phenomenon. The current quest to identify the star of Bethlehem with the movements of Jupiter can be traced to Johannes Kepler, whose planetary calculations are the basis of modern astronomy. Kepler believed that Herod's death was around 4 BC, so he looked for astronomical signs prior to that date. In 1614 he determined that there was a triple conjunction of Jupiter and Saturn in 7 BC and a massing of Jupiter, Saturn, and Mars in 6 BC. Both of these planetary interactions are often presented as contenders (either on their own or together) for the Bethlehem star.[11] Kepler himself postulated that the star was actually a *supernova* in 4 BC, which was caused by Jupiter's

---

10. Allers and Minkoff, *Lion King.*

11. For example, Bulmer-Thomas ("Star of Bethlehem," 363–74) argues that the magi followed Jupiter's retrograde path beginning with the three conjunctions of Jupiter and Saturn in 7 BC, then the massing of Jupiter, Saturn, and Mars in 6 BC, and finally Jupiter's reappearance from behind the sun in May 5 BC.

conjunctions in 7 BC and massing in 6 BC.[12] While there aren't historical records of Kepler's supernova, others have connected the star with novae recorded by the Chinese in 5 BC and the Koreans in 4 BC.[13]

Alternatively, those who assume Herod died in 1 BC often connect the star with Jupiter's bright conjunction with Venus in 2 BC and sometimes the triple conjunctions of Jupiter and the star Regulus in 3–2 BC. For example, Ernest Martin argues Jupiter had two conjunctions with Venus, which bookended the three times that Jupiter obscured Regulus in 3–2 BC. He also claims Jupiter stopped over Bethlehem on December 25, 2 BC, when the magi would have visited Jesus. Frederick Larson's movie, *The Star of Bethlehem*, has popularized a similar (but slightly different) view as Martin. The main problem with these theories is that they rely upon an inaccurate date of Herod's death.[14]

A more convincing and less complicated theory has been argued at least since the time of Origen (*Against Celsus* 1.58). The star is likely a comet appearing in 5 or 4 BC. We should note that this comet was not Halley's Comet, which was visible in 12 BC. The strength of this theory is that other ancient authors describe comets using similar terms as Matthew's description of the star including "rising," "going before," and "standing over" places.[15] Some dismiss this theory claiming that we don't have clear indicators of a comet appearing during this time; however, Chinese records cite comets in 5 BC and 4 BC.[16]

While modern astronomers continue to offer explanations, we need to remember that these cannot definitively prove or disprove Matthew's account. There is a limit to what our astrological models can show us because we have to compare and interpret them with the limited records that tell us

12. It is a popular misunderstanding that Kepler thought the conjunction was the star (Steel, *Marking Time*, 325–26). A modern case for a supernova is made by Morehouse, "Christmas Star as a Supernova," 66–68.

13. Kidger, *Star of Bethlehem*; Clark, Parkinson, and Stephenson, "Nova in 5 BC," 443–49.

14. Martin's *Star of Bethlehem* influences Chester, "Star of Bethlehem," 1–6, who influences Larson, *Star of Bethlehem*. Nicholl ("What Is Wrong with Rick Larson's 'Star'") provides an accessible critique.

15. For example, comets are described with the similar expressions "rising" (*epitolē*, Diodorus Siculus 1.81.5; 2.30.5), "going before" (*proēgeomai*, Diodorus Siculus 16.66.3), and "standing over" (*histēmi*; Dio Cassius, *Roman History* 54.29; Josephus, *Jewish War* 6.289).

16. Humphreys, "Star of Bethlehem—a Comet in 5 BC," 389–407; Nicholl, *Great Christ Comet*.

how ancient people interpreted the heavenly signs. Further, these models can't show us all the phenomena like shooting stars or comets that might have sporadically been displayed in the night sky.

Finally, we need to remember the high level of speculation and subjectivity that remains in such "scientific" models. Astrologers spend their lives observing the stars, and each year hundreds of signs appeared. Can we really narrow down a specific sign to a particular day or year? The fact that these magi saw the star as a sign, but the religious leaders and Herod did not, reveals a bit of the subjectivity.

Stars in the Bible

As we consider the star of Bethlehem, we also need to understand that we approach stars and the cosmos from a different worldview than people in the ancient world. It may be helpful to look at the imagery of stars in the Bible.

Early Christians, such as Justin Martyr, Irenaeus, and Origen, considered the star to be a fulfillment of Balaam's prophecy in Numbers 24:17, which says, "A star shall come out of Jacob, and a scepter shall rise out of Israel." This prophecy pointed to King David's conquest of the nations of Edom and Moab and was considered to foreshadow the future Messiah. Matthew may be making a connection between God using the pagan prophet (or magus) Balaam and God using these pagan magi to fulfill this prophecy.[17]

We also discover that stars were often used as images for angels. For example, Revelation 1:20 says, "The seven stars are the angels of the seven churches." Even today, we understand the personification of stars. Thus, I live in the bright lights and big city of Los Angeles. It's a city full of (movie) stars. But when I look up in the night sky, I'm lucky if I spot even a few actual stars. Whenever I travel out of the city, I'm stunned by the number of stars in the night sky.

Could it be that the magi really did follow a "star" that ultimately rested upon the house where Jesus dwelt? Could it be that just as angels directed the shepherds toward Jesus that an angelic star also guided the wise men?[18] While we may not know for certain, this reading works with

17. Philo (*Life of Moses* 1.50) calls Balaam a magus. Other parallels with the story include Balak, who wants to destroy the Israelites (Numbers 22–24). Hagner, *Matthew*, 1:25.

18. The Arabic Gospel of the Infancy 7 (which is at least from the seventh or eighth century) understood the star to be an angel.

the images of the star's movements including "rising," "going before," and "standing over" in Matthew 2:2 and 2:9.

In the ancient world, the heavenly bodies, including the stars, were connected with celestial beings. It also was thought that the events of the heavens could impact the events on the earth. The divide that we make between a heavenly phenomenon and an angel may not be as neat and tidy as we like.

So, I'm sorry to break it to you, but I can't give you a definitive answer about what this star was. The benefit of seeing this star as a heavenly sign like Jupiter or a comet helps to remind us that the magi were astrologers who looked to the heavens for signs. The benefit of seeing the star as an angel reminds us that these astrologers lived within a worldview that believed that the heavens were filled with spiritual forces that impacted lives here on earth.

I think we are left with several plausible options that allow us to believe Matthew was accurately recounting this story. If you're more scientifically inclined, then go nuts over investigating the various astronomical options. Just remember that anyone who uses these to predict a precise time and date is just speculating and that we don't have any evidence for Jesus being born in December. If you're someone who appreciates literary connections, then seeing the star as an angel may be a more satisfying answer.

The magi were looking into the heavens for guidance about life here on the earth. And when they looked, they found signs pointing to the savior of the world. Do we make our world too small by focusing upon only our own lives, or do we look beyond ourselves to see the ways that God may be working in the world? Can we expand our eyes to look with wonder for the signs of God's work in creation? Do we see God's fingerprints in the beauty of a sunset or the majesty of a meteor shower?

John 3:16 tells us that God loves the whole world, that is, all people. In Romans 8, Paul casts an even wider vision for us that God is in the business of saving all of creation! And Revelation 21–22 ends with a vision of the new heaven and new earth. What would happen if we captured a bit of this grander vision? Would we be willing to follow the signs God put in our lives wherever they take us?

Baby or Toddler Jesus?

But how old was Jesus when they visited? I can't count the number of times that I've been in a Christmas program where there is a pause for weighing the authenticity of the performance after the shepherds' visit. This authenticity is measured by how the directors answer this question: Will the wise men visit the baby Jesus or toddler Jesus?

Very often I've seen the baby Jesus carried off and then replaced by a toddler. I've even been the culpable parent at my church. Of course, I said, "Yes!" when my own son was asked to play the role of two-year-old Jesus waiting to receive his three gifts from the three magi of gold, frankincense, and myrrh.

Those "in the know" wisely point out that in Luke, the shepherds come to visit Jesus on the night of his birth where they see him lying in the manger (Luke 2:16). Luke also recounts Jesus's circumcision eight days later and his presentation in the temple forty days later (Luke 2:21–23).

"Clearly" Jesus had to be a toddler when the magi visited because Matthew calls Jesus a "child" (Greek, *paidion*, Matthew 2:8–9, 11, 13–14, 20–21) not a "baby" (Greek, *brephos*). Also, he is living in a "house" (Greek, *oikia*) in Matthew 2:11. And Herod killed all children under two (Matthew 2:16), which shows that Jesus could have lived in Bethlehem for a few years.

But here's the thing, we really don't know how old Jesus was. In fact, we have early church traditions that portray Jesus both as a baby and as a two-year-old when the wise men visit.[19] Certainly, the assumption that Jesus is under two broadly makes sense in light of Herod's attempt to kill all children under this age.[20] It's been estimated that Herod would have murdered around twenty children in this horrific act.[21]

Those who have lost a loved one and are grieving during Christmas may identify with the pain these families experienced at the loss of their children. The inclusion of these tragic deaths in the Christmas story creates space for those mourning during the Christmas season. Are you

---

19. The Infancy Gospel of James portrays Jesus as a baby, while Pseudo-Julius Africanus's *Fragment on the Incarnation* describes him as a two-year-old. See also Eusebius, *Questions to Stephanus* 16.2. Augustine (*Sermon* 203.1) argued their visit was after the thirteenth day of his birth, which helped link the festival of Epiphany with the magi.

20. Like Matthew's story of the killing of the children, according to Suetonius (*Augustus* 94.2), the Roman senate tried to stop the raising of children in the year that Augustus was born.

21. Hagner, *Matthew*, 1:37. Bethlehem's population was about one thousand.

experiencing grief or loss? What do you need in order to be comforted? Are we looking for the pain and loss of others? How can we bring comfort to those who grieve?

We should also take a moment to consider how the ignorance and foolishness of the magi cost these children their lives. It's a good reminder that good intentions are not always enough. "I meant well" isn't an excuse. Ignorance can be harmful, and we should continue to educate ourselves to help us avoid these kinds of tragedies, especially when it comes to the unborn, babies, and children.

Jesus living in Bethlehem for two years in Matthew would appear different from Luke's portrayal of Jesus being taken to Nazareth forty days after his birth. Luke writes, "When they had finished everything required by the law of the Lord, they returned to Galilee, to their own town of Nazareth" (Luke 2:39).

Further, the supposedly problematic Greek words aren't actually problems. The Greek word for "child" (*paidion*, Matthew 2:8–9, 11, 13–14, 20–21)[22] is also used to describe baby Jesus when he was born (Luke 2:17), when he was eight days old (Luke 2:21), and when he was forty days old (Luke 2:27, 40). So, a "child" (*paidion*) can also be understood as a "baby."

Matthew's reference to a "house" (Greek, *oikia*, Matthew 2:11) actually confirms Luke's description that Mary and Joseph were staying in their extended family's home (Luke 2:7). Further, "after Jesus was born" (Matthew 2:1) is probably not meant to indicate a vast amount of time passing. Rather, this expression serves as a transitional statement to tie the story of the magi into the previous verse that tells of Jesus's birth (Matthew 1:25).

Matthew includes an escape to Egypt (Matthew 2:13–15, 19–23) before moving to Nazareth. Matthew describes the flight to Egypt in a manner that parallels the Old Testament stories of Moses. Just as Pharaoh tried to kill baby Moses, so Herod tries to kill baby Jesus (Exodus 1:22; 2:15; Matthew 2:13–16). After God reveals that Pharaoh/Herod was dead, Moses/Jesus could return safely (Exodus 2:23; 4:19–20; Matthew 2:19–21).[23]

The reason for the family's move to Nazareth was because they did not want to live anywhere in the region of Judea ruled by Herod's cruel son, Archelaus. So, if we try to fit Matthew's and Luke's stories together, we

---

22. We should also note that "little child" (*paidion*) is the diminutive form of "child" (*pais*).

23. Brown (*Birth of the Messiah*, 113–15) also notes parallels in Philo's *Life of Moses* and Josephus's *Antiquities* 2.9.205–37.

discover that we really don't know how old Jesus was in Matthew. Matthew is more likely portraying the magi's visit sometime shortly after his birth but prior to his move to Nazareth.[24]

So, it is quite possible that both the shepherds and the magi had the opportunity to visit baby Jesus. Our historical knowledge of "what actually happened" does not need to distance us from these Christmas stories—whether they portray these magi visiting baby Jesus or the toddler Jesus.

Watching Christmas programs over the years, I'll admit that my favorite versions have always been my kids' kindergarten performances. I'll grant that part of this just has to do with being a proud parent watching the organized chaos of kids dressed in pillowcases singing with tone-deaf gusto about the Christmas story. But part of me loves these programs because they have both the shepherds and wise men visit baby Jesus.

Maybe we need to be a bit more like our kindergarten kids. Maybe we need to be willing to approach Jesus without all of our adult pretentiousness and self-consciousness. Can we approach Jesus with the simple preparation of a child in a pillowcase or the child who unknowingly is picking his or her nose?

Lessons from the Lowly

A natural human tendency is to think positively about ourselves while thinking less of those we disagree with. We can see this tendency in our reading of Herod and the magi. Of course, God doesn't reveal himself to Herod and the religious leaders! After all, Herod tries to kill baby Jesus while the religious leaders will be part of the events that kill the adult Jesus. It's easy to villainize these people. When we do so, we feel superior about ourselves because at least we "get Jesus." We didn't miss the Christmas message.

But the magi are our heroes in the story, so we want them to be as "good" of characters as possible. Because of this, we like the images of three kings, three ambassadors, or even three wise men. We tend to reinforce these kinds of images in our popular imaginations with our Christmas songs and Christmas programs.

In fact, some of us may find it uncomfortable to associate these men with astrologers. Isn't astrology evil, or at least superstitious, since it relies upon a premise that the heavenly bodies can somehow affect our lives here on earth? When I call them astrologers, do modern images of horoscopes

24. This also fits with the early harmonization done by the Infancy Gospel of James.

or Ouija boards come to mind? Surely, the Bible can't say that "these" kind of people sought and found Jesus.

But why not?

It seems that a consistent message of the New Testament is that Jesus came to the earth to seek and to save *the lost*. If we allow the stories of Daniel to influence our understanding of the magi, then it's possible that Matthew is telling a story of redemption. The heirs of the men who stood in opposition to Daniel and his God now seek out his God and pay homage to the Messiah of Israel. The story of the magi becomes a story of encouragement for anyone who knows someone who seems "far away from God." The story of the magi offers a word of encouragement that God really does draw everyone to Jesus.

It turns out that the contrast between Herod and the magi is not really about the relative sinfulness of the people seeking Jesus. Rather, it is about the motivations for seeking Jesus out. Herod sought Jesus in order to secure his own power and position. He sought Jesus in order to destroy him. In contrast, the magi sought Jesus in order to pay homage and to worship him. Herod and the magi can reveal our motivations. They give us a choice of whether we will accept or reject Jesus. Do we seek Jesus for our own status and security, or are we willing to risk our status and security as we seek him out in order to submit to him?

The story of Herod and the magi is a reminder that God chose to reveal his Son not to the elite but to the outsiders and despised. Both went looking for Jesus, but only one group found him.

Let's never grow tired of looking for Jesus.

Reflection Questions

1. Do you have anything special that you want for Christmas? What have been some of your favorite gifts? How do you figure out what to give to others for Christmas? Why do you think the magi gave Jesus gold, frankincense, and myrrh?

2. The magi may have learned about the Messiah from the Jewish descendants of Jews like Daniel who had been taken into exile in Babylon. Has God ever used a difficult event in your life to help others?

3. Why do you think the magi asked Herod for the location of Jesus's birth? The magi's encounter with Herod led to the death of the infants.

Are we responsible for unintentional consequences? How do we avoid hurting others with our good intentions?

4. The magi's story engages with the division between Jews and gentiles. Where do we see our world divided into "us versus them" stereotypes like Jews versus gentiles? How does the story of the magi help us connect racial reconciliation as part of the gospel? How can we stand against racism today and promote justice and reconciliation?

5. A consistent message of the New Testament is that Jesus came to the earth to seek and to save *the lost*. If the magi are astrologers, then how are these magi unworthy and unlikely people who bear witness to Jesus's birth? How does this story challenge our categories of worthy and unworthy?

6. What do you think is the best explanation for the Christmas star? Is it Jupiter, a comet, an angel, or the fulfillment of Numbers 24:17? What are signs of God working in the world today?

7. The ancient world connected heavenly events with earthly events. How do we look for spiritual things in our lives today?

8. How can we follow the magi's example of persistently looking for Jesus?

Activity: Generosity

The magi were known for giving gifts to Jesus. Are there ways that we can give gifts like the magi? Through gift giving, we release our possessions over to God and others. When we have our hands open from giving things away, our hands become free to receive further blessings from God. Keep your eyes open for opportunities to give to others. Maybe you have the chance to bless someone who wasn't expecting a gift. Could you surprise someone by anonymously buying a drink or a meal? We can also give gifts through our words. Who is someone that you could give extra praise to today? What are other gifts that you could give?

10

Ruining a Good Story by Making It Too Long—Rediscovering Why It Was Worth the Wait

H ave you ever sat through a movie that was just too long? How about a book? Have any of us failed in our attempts to read *War and Peace*? There is a famous fantasy book series called the *Wheel of Time*, which was so long that the author, Robert Jordan, actually died before it was finished![1]

One of the keys to good storytelling is not to make the story too long or too short. This will depend upon the ability of the storyteller and the worthiness of the story. While I could tell you about the time that I

---

1. While Robert Jordan died in 2007, thanks to Brandon Sanderson, the series was completed in 2013.

vacuumed my house to clean it before a party, you probably wouldn't want me to. On the other hand, you have been reading this book for a while now. Hopefully, it hasn't been a disappointment.

As we've already noted, Mark's Gospel doesn't even bother to tell the story of Jesus's birth. While both Matthew and Luke are responsible for telling us the birth stories, Luke's Gospel gives the longest account.

The Gospel of Luke is especially noteworthy for bookending his stories of the birth of Jesus with two sets of elderly figures. And both sets of elderly people are connected with prophecies and the temple. First, Luke recounts the story of the surprise pregnancy of Elizabeth and Zechariah along with the birth of their son, John the Baptist. Second, he concludes with a story of Simeon and Anna, who were both waiting for the birth of Israel's savior.

Elizabeth and Zechariah

Just as origin stories and reboots are popular today, so Luke's Gospel offers a retelling of the birth stories of Jesus that includes an origin story. In Luke's retelling, he decides to tell the story-behind-the-story by recounting the birth of Jesus's forerunner, John the Baptist.

John's parents were Zechariah and Elizabeth. They were an elderly couple that could not get pregnant (Luke 1:5–25, 39–80). This couple had spent their entire lives hoping, dreaming, and trying to have a family. But as they neared the latter portion of their lives, they had given up.

Have you ever waited for something? What's your level of patience like? I'm not talking about questions of immediate gratification like, can I wait to eat my dessert until after I've had dinner? I'm talking about big life decisions. How long do we wait until we date someone or marry someone? How long will we wait to have kids? Do we have the patience to save money to buy a car or house? How long are we willing to wait and endure before we give up on our dreams?

It's one thing to wait for things when we live in decent or good circumstances, but it's another thing when the very place where we are waiting hurts us. How long have we endured a bad boss or a bad relationship? Have we ever been faced with a chronic or death-dealing illness? Are there things about our family, neighborhood, or society for which we are agonizing for change?

Like this couple, the people of God had been waiting for what seemed like too long to wait for God to act. The nation of Israel had been looking for a savior, but year after year, they were disappointed. And while they waited, they had to live under corrupt leadership. The renewed hope of Zechariah and Elizabeth was meant to inspire the hope that God had not forgotten his people and was ready to act.

I'm particularly fond of the name "Elizabeth" because my wife's name is the shortened version, "Lisa." Elizabeth's (a.k.a. Lisa's) name means "God is an oath." This name reminds readers of Elizabeth's story that God will be faithful to this couple. If God can keep his promises to this elderly couple, then he can keep his promises to us.

The story of Zechariah and Elizabeth would remind Jewish readers that the nation of Israel was also started by an elderly couple who couldn't get pregnant. Genesis tells us that Abraham and Sarah had to wait until Abraham was one hundred years old and Sarah was ninety years old before Isaac was born (Genesis 17:17; 21:5).

We sometimes forget that God first made his promise to a childless Abraham when he was seventy-five (Genesis 12:4). God told Abraham, "I will make you a great nation" (Genesis 12:2). Later, God told him that his descendants would be as abundant as the stars (Genesis 15:5). Abraham spent twenty-five years waiting for God to act. As he waited on God, Abraham came up with various solutions to get God off the hook for this promise. He tried appointing a member of his clan, Eliezer, as his heir (Genesis 15). When that didn't work, he had a child, Ishmael, with another woman, Hagar (Genesis 16).

The preposterousness of Isaac's birth is verbalized when the near ninety year old Sarah hears the angelic announcement that she will soon have a son, she laughs (Genesis 18:11–15; 21:6). Her laughter could also be her painful response to all the years that she had waited for God to show up and act upon his promise. To commemorate this absurd scene, Abraham names his son "Isaac," which means "laughter" (Genesis 21:3–6).

Luke tells a similar story of a surprise pregnancy.[2] But this time, it is the husband, Zechariah, who does not believe the angelic message (Luke 1:18). Luke 1:8–10 tells us that Zechariah was a priest serving in the temple. In those days, there were about eight thousand priests, so the priests served on a rotation. This was part of Zechariah's week of temple service that he performed twice a year (1 Chronicles 23:6; 24:7–18; 28:13;

---

2. Themes of the impossible nature of Isaac's birth due to Abraham and Sarah's age (Genesis 17:17; 18:10–12) are reflected in the story of Zechariah and Elizabeth. The naming of Isaac involves Abraham following God's command (Genesis 17:19), which parallels the naming of both John and Jesus, following God's command.

Ezra 2:36–39; 10:18–22; Nehemiah 13:30).[3] The chance to enter into the holy place to offer incense was a once in a lifetime opportunity (*Mishnah Tamid* 5:2—6:3; cf. Psalm 141:2), and he is understandably surprised when he encounters an angel.

Zechariah's name means "remembered by Yahweh." With a note of irony, the angel Gabriel[4] tells him that God has remembered his prayers (Luke 1:13). Zechariah's story offers encouragement to anyone who has prayed for something for a

really

long

time.

Zechariah's initial reaction to the angel is disbelief (Luke 1:18). When he asks how the pregnancy would be possible, the angel does not explain to him "the birds and the bees." Instead, the angel gives him a sign by striking him mute for nine months.[5] I'm guessing Zechariah wished he'd kept his mouth shut! While he is unable to speak during Elizabeth's pregnancy (Luke 1:20), after naming his child John, his first words are praises to God (Luke 1:64). And after seeing God fulfill the angel's prophetic word, he utters a prophecy about his son (Luke 1:67–79).

Luke intersperses this account of John's birth with the story of Jesus's birth. He does this to create a "good to great" comparison between John and Jesus.[6] John's birth, like the birth of Isaac, was a miracle because God opened the womb of an elderly couple. Jesus's birth was even more spectacular because Mary was a young virgin. Likewise, John's ministry would foreshadow Jesus's ministry. God did good things through John, but he would do great things through Jesus. These stories give encouragement to people of all ages. God is never through with us, and God values both the young and old alike.

3. The priests were divided into twenty-four courses on duty twice a year. See Josephus's description in *Antiquities* 7.14.7 and *Life* 1. Nolland, *Luke*, 1:35.

4. Gabriel appears in Daniel 8–12 and is also portrayed as one of the seven (Revelation 8:2, 6; 1 Enoch 20; Testament of Levi 8; Tobit 12:15) or four (1 Enoch 9.1; 40.2) angels standing in God's presence.

5. An alternative theory sees Zechariah's silence as an apocalyptic motif where God's plans are hidden from humans until the appropriate time (Daniel 8:26; 12:4, 9; Revelation 10:4). His unbelief also contrasts Mary's belief (Luke 1:45). Nolland, *Luke*, 1:33.

6. The "good to great" motif is commonly observed by commentators. For example, see Nolland (*Luke*, 1:34–35), who parallels their births being foretold (Luke 1:5–25; 1:26–38; 1:39–56; 2:41–52), their births (1:57–66; 2:1–21), and their prophecies (1:67–80; 2:22–40).

What are our hopes and dreams? Where have we expected God to act, but we've felt disappointed because God didn't show up? How patient are we? The story of Elizabeth and Zechariah reminds us to be expectant for God to act. God transforms their lifetime of shame, caused through infertility, into joy. The story of Elizabeth and Zechariah also reminds us that God's plans aren't always our plans. Is it really ideal to have a baby when you're the age of being a grandparent? No. But, this couple provides an example of openness and a willingness to follow God's direction in their lives.

In today's age, we talk about retirement plans. But do we really retire from serving God like we retire from our jobs? Do we think the church must give back a good "Return On Investment" (ROI) after contributing a lifetime of service? Or do we see our final years as a prime opportunity to ask God what is next?

As a church, do we communicate value to the elderly? Are we always asking them to adjust and make sacrifices for the next generation? What if the next generation served the elderly? What if the church had the counter cultural message of valuing both the young and old? What if we were intergenerational communities that did not pit the young versus the old? What if there was a place for the youthful energy of wide-eyed optimism alongside the wisdom gained from the elderly's experience? What if both groups were assets to each other?

Jesus Is Presented at the Temple

Following Jewish customs, Jesus was circumcised and named eight days after his birth (Luke 2:21). While circumcision is practiced in many countries for health and hygiene reasons, we are told in Scripture that this was the sign of God's covenant (or promise) with Israel.[7] Abraham, the father of Israel, was given this sign when he was ninety-nine, and Ishmael was thirteen (Genesis 17:24–25). Isaac is the first official Israelite baby who was circumcised (Genesis 21:4).

It is significant that this sign involves the male reproductive organ. It reminded the Israelites that any children produced are a result of God's promise to make Israel a great nation (Genesis 17:1–21).[8] This sign links

7. Circumcision was also practiced by other nations, possibly including Egypt, Edom, Amon, and Moab (Jeremiah 9:25–26). Herodotus 2.37, 104 claims Egyptian origins of circumcision.

8. Hall, "Circumcision," 1:1025–31.

God's promises and blessings with sex. Do we approach sex and children from the perspective that these are blessings from God? Do we share the pain of those who want, but cannot have, children? Would this change our attitudes and conversations about these things? The Bible does not shy away from talking about sex. Do we?

Because circumcision was an "everlasting covenant" between God and the Jewish people (Genesis 17:13), it makes sense that Jesus would be circumcised. Paul notes that Jesus was "born under the law" (Galatians 4:4). Hebrews 2:17 writes, "He had to become like his brothers and sisters in every respect." In contrast, non-Jewish believers gain access to this sign of circumcision through Christ's circumcision (Colossians 2:11).

Forty days later, Mary and Joseph present Jesus at the temple. According to the Old Testament, the firstborn male is dedicated to God (Exodus 13:2, 12, 16; 34:19; Numbers 18:15–16). In addition, they perform the rights of purification. According to Leviticus 12:11, a woman is purified forty days after childbirth. The traditional offering was a lamb and a young pigeon or dove (Leviticus 12:2–4, 6, 8). However, Mary and Joseph sacrifice of "a pair of turtledoves or two young pigeons" (Luke 2:24). Their sacrifice indicates that Jesus's family was poor enough that they could not afford the full offering.

By highlighting their sacrifice, Luke links Jesus's future ministry to the poor (Luke 4:18–19; Isaiah 61:1–2) with his own family's poor status. In the first century, most of the wealth was concentrated in the top 10 percent of the population. However, Joseph's family would have fit in the lower middle portion of the remaining 90 percent of the population.[9] This aligns with the Gospels' description of Joseph as an artisan worker.

Speaking of Joseph's job, we're actually not sure about Joseph's profession. It turns out that the Greek word *tektōn* (Mark 6:3; Matthew 13:55) can be translated as "carpenter" or "stoneworker."[10] However, the tradition of Joseph's carpentry skills was carried into the second century. In the non-biblical account of the Infancy Gospel of Thomas, we learn that Joseph was not the best carpenter. He apparently did not learn the old adage

9. On the poverty scale, see Friesen, "Poverty in Pauline Studies," 323–61; Longenecker, "Exposing the Economic Middle," 243–78. Using Friesen's numbers, we can break the 90 percent down further. Probably 22 percent of people like merchants, traders, and small farmers lived above subsistence level, while 40 percent of people like laborers and artisans lived at subsistence level, and the final 28 percent lived below subsistence like widows, orphans, beggars, and day laborers.

10. Vaughn, "Carpenter," 1:570.

"measure twice, cut once" because there is a story told of Joseph cutting a board too short. Thankfully, he had Jesus around, and Jesus miraculously lengthened the board for him! (I probably would have asked Jesus to make the whole bed miraculously.)

Regardless of whether Jesus grew up learning how to be a woodworker or a stonemason, he was raised to be an artisan. Joseph and Mary did not distinguish between Jesus being the Messiah and his vocation as a carpenter. Too often we can feel that we need to choose between our religious life and our professional life. For Jesus, this wasn't an either-or choice. Instead, he was both a carpenter and the Messiah. This is a good reminder that God can use us wherever we are and with whatever job we have. We can ask ourselves how can our training and vocation be used by God today?

Simeon and Anna

During this visit to the temple, Jesus's family encounters two other elderly people, Simeon and Anna, who had been waiting their entire lives to see the salvation of Israel (Luke 2:22–38).[11] These two characters are often neglected in our Christmas pageants. On the one hand, Luke does not give Simeon's age, but the non-biblical account of The Gospel of Pseudo-Matthew 15:2 gives him the age of 112! On the other hand, Luke apparently has not been told that it is impolite to tell an elderly woman's age, so we are told that Anna is at least eighty-four years old (Luke 2:37).

These two elderly people had waited their entire lives to see the salvation of Israel. First, Jesus's family encounters Simeon (Luke 2:25–35). Simeon is described as a "righteous" and "pious" man who was waiting for the Messiah. Just as the angels had told the shepherds that Jesus brings peace (Luke 2:14), Simeon praises God that he can now die in peace because he has seen Jesus. Simeon can die in peace because God has kept his word.

After seeing Jesus, Simeon praises God for the upcoming salvation for both Jews (fulfilling passages like Isaiah 42:6; 46:13; 49:6; 52:9–10) and non-Jews (fulfilling passages like Isaiah 2:2–3 and Micah 4:1). But besides a blessing, Simeon also utters a warning to Mary that Jesus would divide the nation in two since he was "destined for the falling and rising of many

---

11. While Malachi 3:1 was used to predict the coming of John the Baptist, Malachi 3:2 may stand behind Jesus's presentation at the temple (Brown, *Birth of the Messiah*, 445). Brown also sees Daniel 9:21–24 behind this story. See also the figures of Eli and Hannah in 1 Samuel 1–2.

in Israel" (Luke 2:34), which is based on Isaiah 8:14–15 and 28:13–16.[12] Further, using imagery of a "sword piercing her soul," Mary is warned that she would feel a mother's pain as she witnessed her son's suffering and rejection throughout his ministry.

Second, the family meets the prophet Anna. She was a widow who remained in the temple fasting and praying (Luke 2:36–38). Widows held a special place in God's heart along with strangers, orphans, and the poor (Exodus 22:21–24).[13] After this encounter, we are told that Anna praised God and spoke about the child to anyone who would listen.

This episode with Anna would help jog the memory of the Old Testament story of Hannah (notice the similar spelling). Hannah was a barren woman who went year after year to the temple to beg God for a child (1 Samuel 1–2). Eventually, God granted her request, and her son, Samuel, was born. She dedicated the child to the Lord's service, and he became the last judge of Israel. Just as Samuel grew up and became strong (1 Samuel 2:26), so Luke tells us that Jesus grew up in God's favor (Luke 2:39–40).[14]

The stories of Zechariah and Anna remind us that God can reward a lifetime of patient service. These two people looked for God to act every day of their lives. They woke up in the morning, expecting God to act. When they went to bed at night, they did not need to be disappointed because they knew one day God would answer their requests. Each day they woke up looking for Christmas. Until one day when they awoke, it really was Christmas! It reminds me of a common saying in Eswatini, "If not today, then tomorrow for sure." Do we expect God to be working if not today, then tomorrow for sure? Are we people who wake up every day looking for God to act?

Keeping the Celebration Going: Advent and Epiphany

What would it look like for us to extend our celebration of Christmas today? One way to begin Christmas early is through the celebration of

---

12. These Old Testament texts are alluded to elsewhere in the New Testament such as Romans 9:33; 1 Peter 2:6–8; Luke 20:17–18.

13. Other passages include Deuteronomy 10:18; 27:19; Jeremiah 49:11; Luke 7:11–15; and so forth. Famous widows included Ruth (Ruth 2:1–23), the widow of Zarephath (1 Kings 17:8–24), and Tabitha (Acts 9:36–43). Thurston, "Widow," 5:847.

14. Echoes of the Samuel story bookend Jesus's birth—Zechariah and Elizabeth's son recalls Samuel, and Anna recalls Hannah.

Advent.[15] "Advent" is from the Latin word *adventus*, which means "coming towards." Advent invites people to reflect upon the "coming" of Jesus in three ways. First, people have the chance to celebrate Jesus's previous coming through his birth. Second, people can look in the present for Jesus's spiritual coming into the lives of believers. Third, people can wait expectantly for Jesus's future return.

Many churches celebrate Advent on the four Sundays before Christmas Day, and Advent season is the beginning of the church year. Traditionally, the season of Advent was a time of waiting and penitence leading up to the celebration of Christmas. In recent times, Advent is emphasized as a season of hope and rejoicing because of Christ's coming.

The Advent wreath was developed by Christians during the Middle Ages. They sought to redeem the practice of northern Europeans (notable in Germany and Scandinavia) who lit winter candles during their winter rites as a sign of hope for the future warmth of spring. The wreath is usually made of evergreens, which represent eternal life. It also features four candles, which can represent hope, peace, joy, and love. Sometimes it includes a fifth candle, which represents Jesus.[16]

Advent reminds us that Christmas doesn't have to focus only upon the past, with our recollections of Jesus's birth. It's a season that prompts us to remember that Jesus is still spiritual present today and working among us. It also extends our gaze into the future by giving us hope. When we experience the brokenness of this world, we find the assurance that Jesus plans to come again in the future to set the world right. With Advent, Christmas expands Christ's coming into our past, present, and future.

Further, our annual Christmas celebrations don't have to be over after December 25! One popular Christmas carol is the "Twelve Days of Christmas." These twelve days are based on the period between the celebration of Christmas on December 25 and the celebration of another Christian holiday called Epiphany on January 6.[17]

Like Christmas, Epiphany probably originated as a Christian alternative to the winter solstice and the sun-god festivals observed. Our

15. O'Shea and Roll, "Advent," 1:133–35; Crump, "Advent," n.p.

16. For more on the Advent wreath and ways to observe Advent, see the appendix.

17. Connell, "Epiphany, The Solemnity of," 5:293–95. See also, Talley, *Origins of the Liturgical Year*, 79–162; Chupungco, *Liturgical Time and Space*, 5:135–330. In the Middle Ages, Twelfth Night was celebrated with music, singing, dancing, masquerades, and so forth. It became the custom to elect a mock king, the lord of Misrule, to supervise the festivities.

earliest record of a January 6 celebration comes from Clement of Alexandria (*Stromateis* 1.21.145–46; AD 215).[18] Other records include the journal of Ammianus Marcellinus (AD 363) and Epiphanius (*Panarion* 51.16; AD 315–403). By the fourth century, Epiphany celebrated the stories of Jesus's birth, the coming of the magi, his baptism, and his first miracle of turning water into wine. "Epiphany" comes from the Greek word meaning "manifestation" and is meant to celebrate the manifestation of Jesus.

In our celebrations of Christmas, do we make the "manifestation" of Jesus clear? If we look beyond Christmas, do we see other ways that Jesus is manifesting himself in the world? Do people only see Jesus when they read their Bibles or go to church? What are the followers of Jesus doing to manifest Jesus in their homes? At work? At school? In society?

We might also ask ourselves how substantive are these manifestations of Jesus? Is Jesus a mere ghost, or does he affect our lives and the lives of others? Do our manifestations of Jesus look like us, or can people tell the difference between Jesus and the church?

Like the stories of Zechariah and Elizabeth as well as Simeon and Anna, we can look for ways to extend the Christmas story into our lives. Thanks to Black Friday sales and generous return policies, we've been taught by our culture to extend the commercialization and consumerism of Christmas. But what if we extended our spiritual reflections on the birth of Jesus?

Practically, we can extend Christmas into the whole month of December leading up to Christmas through Advent. Further, we can extend Christmas into January through the twelve days of Christmas leading up to Epiphany. But the birth of Jesus doesn't have to be celebrated only during the winter season. Just as the early Christians celebrated Jesus's conception around March 25, we can extend our celebrations to earlier times of the year.

But why be limited to just these dates? Why not remember Jesus's birth throughout the whole year? Are there other things that can remind us of Jesus's birth? What if when we see the birth of a child or celebrate our own birthdays, we also remember the birth of Christ? Maybe the next time we say, "Happy birthday," to each other; we can also say, "Happy birthday, Jesus!"

---

18. Although, Clement of Alexandria notes heretical Christians, called the Gnostics, celebrated it.

Reflection Questions

1. What's one of the longest movies that you've watched or books that you've read? Do you wish the Christmas stories were longer? What additional information would you like to know? Why do you think Luke added the stories of Zechariah, Elizabeth, Simeon, and Anna?

2. While Zechariah and Elizabeth had given up their dream to have a baby, God had not forgotten them. What are your hopes and dreams? Have you ever waited for something for a really long time? Are there prayers that you are still waiting to hear answered? Are there things about our family, neighborhood, or society for which we are agonizing for change?

3. Simeon and Anna persistently went to the temple because they believed in God's promises. How can we wake up every day looking for God to act?

4. Luke's stories remind us that God values the young and old. How can the church have the counter-cultural message of valuing both the young and old? How can we create intergenerational communities that help both groups be assets to each other?

5. Luke connects the naming of Jesus with his circumcision. What can Jewish circumcision teach us about God's promises and blessings when it comes to sex, children, and families? Are there ways that we can have more open, honest, and godly conversations about sex?

6. Joseph and Mary's purification offering indicates that Jesus's family was part of the 90 percent of the world that was poor. How do you think Jesus identifies with the poor of the world today? How can the church help the poor without being paternalistic?

7. When raising Jesus, Joseph and Mary did not distinguish between Jesus as a carpenter and the Messiah. How can God use our training and vocation to minister to others?

8. Just as Luke extends the birth stories, what are ways that we can extend our celebration of Christmas throughout the year? Does your family or church celebrate Advent or Epiphany?

Activity: Giving Something Up

Fasting, or giving something up, may appear out of place in a book on Christmas. However, fasting can help teach us the patience needed as we wait for the promises of God like the elderly people mentioned in this chapter. Fasting is an opportunity to make space for God in our lives by removing something that we've grown dependent upon. Fasting can take a variety of forms. People have been known to skip a meal, abstain from certain drinks, not eat during the daytime, or give something up like TV or social media. What could you give up for a short period of time in order to teach gratitude for God's provisions as well as patience while you wait for God to provide?

11

Ruining Xmas—Rediscovering Christmas

I don't think I'm alone in having mixed feelings about mall Santas.

As a parent, I remember being excited to share the magic of Christmas by taking my kids to the mall to let them sit on Santa's lap, get a picture, and share their Christmas wishes. It's supposed to be fun and festive!

Until we realized that we had an hour to wait in line . . .

because mom and dad were too cheap . . .

and came on the day where photos with Santa were . . .

free.

My wife and I had a real sense of accomplishment when we managed to distract and bribe our four kids (all under eight) all the way to the front of the line. Then, it was finally time to sit on Santa's lap . . .

. . . and that was when one of my kids started to scream and cry.

Here Comes Santa Claus . . .

So where did all this Santa business start? And can I be a good Christian and still have fun with Santa? Does Santa ruin Christmas?

Our modern images of Santa and Mrs. Claus portray them as a kindly elderly couple waiting to bestow gifts on all the good little girls and boys. Santa sometimes goes by other names such as Saint Nicholas, Kris Kringle, or Father Christmas.

Dressing up as Santa often involves donning a white beard and wig, a red hat and coat, and possibly stuffing a pillow under our shirt. When Tim Allen became the "new" Santa Claus in his movie, *The Santa Clause*, he gained the appropriate amount of weight and white hairs.

Santa was introduced into the Christmas season through the historical figure of Saint Nicholas (AD 270–343).[1] Nicholas was a Christian bishop in Myra, which is located in modern-day Turkey. Nicholas was known for his secret gift-giving to the poor. One of the most well-known legends about him involved rescuing three girls from prostitution by providing the money for their dowry. (Saint Nick was anti-human trafficking.)

In the Middle Ages, children were given gifts in his honor the evening before his feast day on December 6. He also became the patron saint of Greece, sailors, brewers, repentant thieves, merchants, and others. As someone who likes to sail, I could become a fan of Saint Nick!

The stories of Saint Nicholas took on new forms through Dutch traditions. Saint Nicholas was known as Sinterklass. He was an elderly man with white hair and a long beard, wore red over his white bishop clothes, and had a white hat. He also possessed a list of naughty and nice children.

Sound familiar?

Each year, he would arrive by boat and ride a white horse to give gifts to children. Children would leave their shoes next to the fireplace with carrots or hay for his horse on December 5. (I think I prefer milk and chocolate chip cookies.) Good children would find candy or small presents in their shoes the next day.

However, naughty kids were caught by his assistant Zwarte Piet. Unfortunately, Zwarte Piet (a.k.a. Black Pete), the dark-skinned companion of Sinterklaas, reminds us that not all Christmas traditions are positive or uncontroversial. People portraying Black Pete usually dress up in blackface and colorful clothing. While some have argued that Pete became black

---

1. Gibson, "Nicholas of Myra, St.," 10:377–78; Gulevich, "Santa Claus," 699–710.

from the soot of a fireplace, the Dutch's history of colonization and their participation in the transatlantic slave trade cannot be disentangled from this tradition.[2] Reflecting upon Zwarte Piet can remind us to examine our own history and traditions and challenge us to be proactive advocates against racism in our own lives and in society.[3]

Our modern ideas of Santa also incorporate traits from the English figure known as Father Christmas, who generally personified the spirit of Christmas and was known from at least the sixteenth century. He was a large man wearing green or scarlet robes and was the spirit of good cheer. When England stopped celebrating the feast day of Saint Nicholas on December 6, the Father Christmas celebration was moved to December 25.[4]

Others see Germanic influences upon Christmas with their midwinter Yuletide celebration. During this time, a long-bearded figure, Wodan, who was equivalent to the Norse god Odin, gave gifts to people as he rode the night sky upon either a horse or reindeer.

Made in America

In America, ideas of Santa Claus may be loosely based on these older traditions. However, they are also the product of years of intentional marketing that began with traditions *created* in the early nineteenth century by wealthy New Yorkers who were part of the New-York Historical Society.

Christmas was part of their project to invent traditions for American society. "Invented traditions" were customs that were made up "with the precise purpose of appearing old-fashioned."[5] The society's founder, John Pintard, was instrumental in establishing numerous national holidays including Washington's birthday, the Fourth of July, and Columbus Day. For more than twenty years, he refined the perfect Christmas holiday that was meant to offset the rowdy celebrations of the poor in New York City.

Another member of the society was Washington Irving, who is known for classics like "Rip Van Winkle" and "The Legend of Sleepy

---

2. McWhorter, "Is 'Black Pete' Racist?" 1; "Is Zwarte Piet Racism? Race Relations in the Netherlands," 58.

3. For example, removing racist mascots as the Washington football team did in 2020.

4. We also see the influence of the Victorian ideas about Christmas through Charles Dicken's *A Christmas Carol* (1843). See the discussion by Barnett, *American Christmas*, 14–18.

5. Nissenbaum, *Battle for Christmas*, x; Hobsbawm and Ranger, *Invention of Tradition*.

Hollow." Irving in his *A History of New-York from the Beginning of the World to the End of the Dutch Dynasty* (1809) describes Saint Nicholas riding in a wagon bearing gifts for children, smoking a pipe, and knowingly pressing his finger against his nose.

Then a friend of Irving, Clement Clarke Moore, anonymously published the poem "The Night Before Christmas" (first called "A Visit from St. Nicholas") on December 23, 1823.[6] This poem included the names of Santa's reindeer—Dasher, Dancer, Prancer, Vixen, Comet, Cupid, Donner, and Blitzen. Rudolf later joined the team over a century later through Gene Autry's 1949 popular song adaptation of the short story "Rudolf the Red-Nosed Reindeer."[7] Autry's voice also introduced the popular figure Frosty the Snowman after the success of his recording of Rudolf.[8] Rudolf's story was turned into a TV special in 1964, which was followed by Frosty's story in 1969.

Our images of Santa with his long white beard, black boots, and red suit draw upon Thomas Nast's illustrations for *Harper's Weekly* from 1863–1886. Nast set Santa's home in the North Pole and included elves as Santa's helpers. The Coca-Cola campaigns from 1931–1964, using the paintings of Haddon Sundblom, further pressed Santa into the popular American imagination.[9]

Can We Save Christmas from Saint Nick?

So what do Christians do with jolly old Saint Nick?

I've been told that one of the greatest villains for ruining Christmas was Santa Claus. After all, if you rearrange the letters of "Santa," you get the word "Satan." Santa can be viewed by detractors as promoting "festal indulgences rather than being a benign gift giver."[10] He is accused of obscuring

6. While first published anonymously, Clement Moore claimed authorship in 1887. Over the years, there have been unproven claims that Henry Livingston wrote it. Keller, "More Things Change," 72–79. Barnet, *American Christmas*, 25–36.

7. The Rudolf story was written by Robert May and first published in 1939 by the department store, Montgomery Ward. Johnny Marks wrote the song, and Gene Autry performed it in 1949.

8. Walter Rollins and Steve Nelson wrote the song, and Gene Autry recorded it in 1950.

9. Coca-Cola has a webpage dedicated to the development of its famous Santa image: www.coca-colacompany.com/stories/coke-lore-santa-claus.

10. Schmidt, *Consumer Rites*, 186.

more than complementing the true Christmas story. These accusations against Santa aren't new. In the early 1900s the *Sunday School Times* wrote that Christmas was not "Santa Claus Day" or "Santamas."[11]

Judge me if you want, but I've never been one of those parents who was willing to let a pretend person take credit for the loving and thoughtful presents that I was going to give to my kids. Nor am I the kind of parent that doesn't think that we can't all enjoy together the pretend story of a jolly old man, his wife, elves, and reindeer.

Just like the Tooth Fairy and the Easter Bunny, my kids have a great time watching dad dress up and pretend in order to bring a little fun and spirit to the season. I also tell my kids not to go around spoiling Christmas or other holidays for the other kids. But for my family, I want them to have a clear sense between stories that are made-up and those that are real. I also want my kids to have fun with their imaginations. But I also want to be aware of the commercial influence upon the Christmas season, and how much of the American celebration of Christmas is rooted in traditions created in the last two hundred years.

The War on Xmas

Because of "issues" like Santa Claus, I grew up believing there was a "war on Christmas." People in my church would wring their hands at all the secularization, commercialization, and commodification of Christmas.

Despite the uptick of Black Friday sales, we knew that Jesus was the "true gift" of Christmas. Advent calendars weren't just the chance for kids to get twenty-four days of chocolates or toys. They were meant to mark the days leading up to Christmas Day. The story of Mary, Joseph, and Jesus was the original Christmas movie. We knew that "Jesus was the reason for the season."

One favorite mantra was "We need to put the 'Christ back into Xmas.'"[12] To replace "Christ" with a simple X seemed to embody the larger social enterprise of keeping the holiday but removing any Christian trappings. Even worse, Christ's name was simply crossed out with an X!

11. Schmidt, *Consumer Rites*, 186.

12. The slogan "Put Christ Back into Christmas" first appeared in a 1949 campaign by the Milwaukee Archconfraternity of Christian Mothers (Schmidt, *Consumer Rites*, 188–91).

Sadly, such comments revealed more about my own ignorance than about commercialization or the conspiracy of non-Christians. It turns out the "X" is simply an abbreviation for the first letter of the Greek name for "Christ," which is Χριστός (*Christos*). So, Xmas is meant to be an abbreviation of Christmas. In reality, we don't need to put Christ back into Xmas because he never left.

Taking the Cross Out of Christmas

However, this abbreviation raises a different issue for me. Notice how the X looks a bit like one form of a Roman cross. In fact, it has been used to symbolize the cross on objects ranging from coins to flags. This X reminds me how often I hear pastors talking about Jesus dying on the cross for our sins during Christmas celebrations.

Reflecting upon Jesus's death during Christmas is not a new phenomenon. Some of the early traditions surrounding Jesus's birth connected the day of his conception as corresponding to the same date of his crucifixion (March 25). Even in our Bible, Zechariah's song praises God for the coming savior who will "forgive people of their sins" (Luke 1:77). Also, Paul joined Jesus's act of becoming human with Jesus's "death on a cross" and heavenly exaltation (Philippians 2:5–11).

So, connecting Jesus's birth with his death is an old, even "biblical" tradition.

I also understand why pastors feel the need to share the events of Jesus's crucifixion during Christmas. In today's culture, there are only a few "windows" where people who are either not Christians or nominal Christians will darken the door of a church. Pastors seek to capitalize on these moments. They want to make sure that they share the message of salvation with people who may not usually hear it.

As my pastor puts it, becoming a Christian is as simple as A.B.C. First, you need to "Accept" that you're a sinner "since all have sinned and fall short of the glory of God" (Romans 3:23). Then, you need to "Believe," that is, to trust, that Jesus can be your savior, since "God so loved the world that he gave his only Son, so that everyone who believes in him may not perish but may have eternal life" (John 3:16). Finally, you need to "Confess" your allegiance to Jesus as your Lord, which is why Paul writes, "If you confess with your lips that Jesus is Lord and believe in your heart that God raised him from the dead, you will be saved" (Romans 10:9).

Oops. I guess I'm also guilty of throwing a salvation message into the Christmas story.

But can you imagine holding someone else's baby boy and saying in one breath, "He is so cute!" However, in the next moment you say, "I'm so glad he is going to be murdered when he is in his thirties!"

Now I think the cross is important, and I'm glad Jesus died for my sins. I'm also glad that sin and death were conquered when God raised Jesus from the dead. However, I also know that we have a whole different holiday where we get to remember Jesus's death and resurrection. It's called Easter. As the church calendar developed in the fourth century, Christmas and Easter became distinct holidays. I wonder if we would benefit by simply letting Christmas be Christmas and letting Easter be Easter?

So, I find it ironic how many Christians who worry about "taking the Christ out of Christmas" end up "putting the cross into Xmas." Isn't the miracle of God becoming a human being mind-blowing enough for us to celebrate? What if we spent the season reflecting on what this means? What does it mean for Jesus to give up his divine privileges to become a human? What does it mean for God to live among us? What does it mean for God to identify with us?

What if God Was One of Us?

Can we stare in wonder at our portraits of the baby Jesus and ask ourselves what it means for God to become one of us? The Gospel of John does this kind of meditation. It replaces the Christmas story with the story of the Word of God, who created the world and became human (John 1:1–18). Or maybe we could meditate upon Hebrews 1:2–4, which describes Jesus as "the reflection of God's glory and the exact imprint of God's very being."

How does the God of the universe become a human? This question may be like asking how do you fit the entire ocean into a cup of water? Or how could a person become an ant? Maybe you've experienced this dilemma when you've packed your bags for an airplane trip and had to squeeze your "life" into a suitcase that weighs under forty or fifty pounds.

Somehow, the essence of God was able to fit into the person of Jesus. But how? Twice the apostle Paul explicitly talks about Jesus becoming a human in Colossians 1:15–20 and Philippians 2:5–11.

First, Paul affirms that Jesus was fully God. Colossians 1:15 and 1:19 remind us that Jesus is "the image of the invisible God" and "in him all the fullness of God was pleased to dwell." Likewise, Philippians 2:6 describes Jesus as being "in the form of God." Second, Paul describes the process of Jesus becoming human when he says that Jesus "emptied himself . . . being born in human likeness. And being found in human form" (Philippians 2:7–8).[13]

Based on passages like these, the Christian church teaches that Jesus is completely God and completely human. When Jesus became human, he had to "empty" or put aside some of his divine attributes. In other words, Jesus put aside or didn't use things like being all-powerful, all-knowing, and all-present when he became human.

It wasn't like Jesus packed his bags into his human suitcase. Then he went to the beach on the Sea of Galilee and realized that he forgot his sunscreen or bathing suit. Instead, Jesus took all the important elements with him and set the rest aside to be picked back up when he returned home. Jesus still possessed all of his divine qualities, but he left some behind for the short period of his earthly life.

According to Colossians 1:20, the reason that Jesus became a human was to bring peace and reconciliation to the world. If my house were infested with ants, I would put out ant poison. But what if I had the ability to become an ant (or Ant-Man) and talk with them to show them where they could get food and water outside my house? Jesus becoming a human is similar to if I could become an ant. It would be a miracle.

We can also draw a connection between God and humans that does not exist between a human and an ant. It is this connection that creates the possibility of God becoming human. The Bible says that God created humans in his image, in his likeness (Genesis 1:26–27). People were made in God's pattern. For example, I can draw your portrait. Then, depending upon my artistic skills, you will either recognize yourself or think that I'm a terrible artist. The Bible says that humans are made in the image of God. We are like his portrait. If we are the image of God, then this makes more sense of how Jesus could become one of us.

If you're stuck trying to figure all this out, don't worry because you're in good company. It took the church around four hundred years, several hundred scholars, and a bunch of major meetings to come up with ways of articulating the concept that Jesus is 100 percent God and 100 percent human in a way that most Christians could agree. And even these agreed upon statements still sound quite confusing. The good news is that if you've

---

13. For more on this hymn, see Martin, *Hymn of Christ*.

ever seen a three-leaf clover or used Italian salad dressing, then you've got a shot at understanding the basics.

First, let's talk clovers. Christians call themselves "monotheist" meaning they claim to believe and worship only one God. However, Christians also believe in the "Trinity," which is the claim that this one God consists of three persons—the Father, Son, and the Holy Spirit.[14] How does that work? How can three persons be one God? This is where clovers come in. Just as one clover has three leaves, so there is one God in three persons. Other analogies include a tree consisting of roots, a trunk, and branches; or an egg having three parts—a yoke, an egg white, and a shell.

As the church grappled with how to describe this triune nature of God, the Council of Nicaea in AD 325 affirmed that Jesus was the same essence as the Father.[15] But this created a bit of a problem for the church. If Jesus was completely God, then how could he also be born as a human to the virgin Mary? So once again, the major leaders of the church called a meeting called the Council of Chalcedon in AD 451. It was at this meeting that leaders said Jesus is like Italian salad dressing.

Anyone who has ever used Italian dressing knows that you need to first vigorously shake up the bottle before pouring it on your salad. That's because Italian dressing is made of a suspension of oil and vinegar, which don't quite mix but are combined to make the dressing. Like a delicious salad dressing, these church leaders said that Jesus has two equal and unmixed natures—he is 100 percent human, and he is 100 percent divine. We even have a fancy name for this idea. It's called the "hypostatic union."

While the clover and salad dressing are imperfect analogies, they get at really important ideas about Jesus. First, the clover helps us to understand how Jesus is fully and completely God. Second, the Italian dressing helps us understand how God could become a human in order to save us. The miracle of Christmas is so big that we are still trying to come up with ways to explain it.

---

14. For reflections on the "Trinity," see various works by Fred Sanders like *The Triune God*. A good, short article is Sanders, "We Actually Don't Need a Trinitarian Revival," n.p.

15. The Pseudo-Athanasian Creed, dated between AD 450–800, clearly articulates the doctrine of the Trinity (Schaff, *Creeds*, 1:35–36). "That we worship one God in Trinity, and Trinity in Unity; neither confounding the Persons: nor dividing the Substance. For there is one Person of the Father: another of the Son: and another of the Holy Ghost" (Schaff, *Creeds*, 2:66).

Becoming Ants

While we can't exactly explain how God became one of us, we can still follow Jesus's example by attempting to step into the shoes of others. What if I tried to consider the point of view of others? And what if we considered their point of view valid? We call this "empathy." Empathy can be described as "the ability to press pause on our own thoughts and feelings long enough to explore someone else's thoughts and feelings."[16]

What if I disagreed with a coworker? Could I see why he or she might be right? What if the next time I'm in a fight with my wife, I try to hear her perspective? Could I assume that just like I have really good reasons for my actions, those with whom I disagree also have their own set of really good reasons?

The world has become an increasingly divided place. My Facebook friends don't act much like friends anymore, especially in the areas of politics and religion. What if Christians acted like Jesus and practiced empathy? Could we put ourselves in other people's shoes for the sake of reconciling our differences? If the God of the universe could figure out how to become a tiny baby boy, could we put some effort into trying to understand the experiences of others?

In addition, Paul challenges his audience to have a humble mindset. According to Philippians 2:7, Jesus "did not regard equality with God as something to be exploited." In other words, Jesus did not take advantage of his relationship with God. Jesus gave up his divine privileges. How often do we focus on our rights and privileges? What would it look like for Christians to give up what we "deserve" on behalf of others? Would we be able to trust that God would exalt us like God "highly exalted Jesus and gave him the name that is above every name"?

As we read the stories of Jesus's birth together, let's not fast-forward to the end of the story. Let's just hang out and exist in these Christmas stories and see what kinds of gift the presence of God has to offer us today. And can we be the presence of God in the lives of others? What would happen if God showed up? What if he's here already?

16. Joiner, "Monday is Coming," n.p.

Reflection Questions

1. Do you have any Santa Claus stories? Maybe you've visited him in the mall, or a family member dresses up as Santa each Christmas. Do you put out socks over your fireplace or set out cookies and warm milk? Do you have a favorite Santa Claus song or movie?

2. In this chapter, we learned that American Christmas traditions like Santa Claus, his reindeer, and his workshop with elves at the North Pole are relatively recent "invented traditions." Why do you think these traditions were made up? Why do you think people put so much effort into getting children to believe in Santa? Do we put the same effort into helping people believe in Jesus? Do made-up stories about Santa lead to children thinking stories of Jesus are made up?

3. Do you think there is a war on Christmas? Do Santa Claus and societies' Christmas celebrations detract or complement the celebration of Jesus's birth?

4. For Christians, Christmas began as a religious celebration of Jesus's birth. What things do you do that put the focus of Christmas upon the birth of Jesus? Do you think churches should have Christmas Eve services, Christmas services, or both? Do churches need to make their Christmas services more attractive?

5. What do you think of the A.B.C. gospel message from this chapter? How would you explain the message of salvation in your own words?

6. Why do Christians believe in the Trinity? How would you explain it to someone else? Do you tend to focus your spiritual relationship with God upon the Father, Jesus, or the Holy Spirit?

7. If Jesus is God, then he gave up a lot of privileges and power in order to become a human. How can we be like Jesus and give us our rights and privileges for others?

8. How can we follow Jesus's model of the incarnation and step into other people's shoes? How do we consider other people's points of view? How can I practice empathy for the sake of reconciling our broken world?

Activity: Service

When the Son of God became a baby boy, he did this to serve humankind. Being a servant puts other's needs before our own. How can we follow Jesus's example of service? We may think service needs to be done in large, grand gestures, but we can also practice service in little ways for those around us. As we take these baby-steps of service, they can help us to take larger and larger steps. Look for little ways to serve others—a kind word or doing a small task. Let these little gestures lead you towards bigger acts of kindness.

12

Conclusion: Ruining Using Christmas—
Rediscovering Enjoying Christmas

Have I ruined Christmas too much for you? Maybe I haven't ruined it enough.

Each year, we let our kids put together our family's nativity set, and each year it looks different. Sometimes Mary is on the right side of baby Jesus. Sometimes she's on the left. Sometimes Joseph is inside the house. Sometimes he's guarding his family on the outside. Some years, all the sheep are flocked together. Other years, they are all huddled around the manger. Some years, the camels stretch across the shelf. Other times, they've completed their journey and are resting outside the stable.

As much as we enjoy our nativity set, we always end up tearing it down and packing it away in bubble wrap for the next year. While there's a sadness when Christmas is over and decorations have to be put away, there's also a sense of anticipation for the next year.

I hope that, like my family's nativity set, this book has been a chance for us to take apart some of our stories about Christmas. We've been able to look carefully and admire the pieces, and then to put our nativity set back together for us to enjoy during the holiday season. And just as we've pulled apart, admired, and put back together the Christmas story, I hope each of us has been able to look within ourselves and see what needs to be challenged, encouraged, and built up.

What Is Love? Baby [Jesus] Don't Hurt Me.

One of my favorite Christian thinkers was a man named Augustine of Hippo. In fact, I liked him so much that we named our oldest son after him. Although our son currently prefers just to be called "Gus," it makes him laugh to link Augustine with a hippo. I still love the name, which means "majestic."

Augustine wrote a little book called *On Christian Teaching*, which opens with a discussion about love. Most people have an innate sense of what love is. We know how to show love for others. We also know when we feel loved by other people. But have you ever tried to define love? It turns out that certain concepts in this world are really big and important, but they are also really hard to pin down. Try to describe the concept of "beauty," "enjoyment," or "good."

To make matters worse, I can say things like, "I love my wife. I love my kids. I love my dog. I love my house. I love pizza," and everyone has a sense of what I mean. Yet, I don't love my wife in the same way that I love pizza. And if I did, you would probably question my sanity. Further, even if we both agreed that we loved pizza, we experience that love for pizza in our own unique ways.

It turns out that in relationships, love is experienced in a variety of ways. One popular approach for understanding "love" comes from Gary Chapman's *5 Love Languages*. He presents two basic premises. First, we all operate out of a primary expression of love. Second, we all give and receive love in a unique combination of ways. Chapman describes the five types of love as the following:

1. Words of affirmation
2. Gift giving and receiving
3. Quality time
4. Acts of service
5. Physical touch

Thus, for some people, love is given and received through words of affirmation. Are you someone who values a compliment? Good for you! For other people, love is given and received through gifts. I know we all like to get stuff! But gift giving is more specific. This may be your love language if you are someone who can spend hours and hours finding just the right gift for a person. It's not your language if your default is to give gift cards. Other people find that love is expressed through the quality time spent together. Do you like to just "hang out" with people, and it really doesn't matter what you're doing? Still others express their love through acts of service. Are you enlivened when you can do something for others? Do you live to do the dishes or to take out the trash? Finally, others feel love most strongly through physical touch. Are you a hugger or a hand-holder?

Problems arise when we try to show love to others using a language they're not using. Have you ever given someone a really nice gift, but they don't seem to appreciate it? Maybe you're in a relationship where you are always doing things for that person, but they simply want to spend time together. Are you always helping other people to do various jobs, but you don't understand why nobody else seems to want to help? Do you always want to shake people's hands or give friendly hugs, but people feel like you're invading their personal space? By understanding your love language, you can figure out ways to experience love as well as how to show love for others.

When you read the Christmas story, which one of these love languages speaks most clearly to you? Do you gravitate toward the words of encouragement spoken by characters like the angelic hosts or Simeon? Maybe you were impressed with the gifts of the magi. Were you challenged by Mary's willing acceptance of her pregnancy as God's servant? Perhaps you contemplated what a special time it must have been for Mary, Joseph, and Jesus on that first Christmas. Or were you struck by how Mary tenderly wrapped Jesus in swaddling clothes?

A Love Like No Other

For Christians, love is a really big deal.[1] Sometimes, people quote 1 John 4:8, which tells us that "God is love." The verse does not say "love is God." By switching this order, we can tend to confuse the value or virtue of love with God. Rather, 1 John tells us that one of the main characteristics of God is his ability to love.

In terms of the Christmas story, we may recall the most famous verse in the Bible, John 3:16, which says, "For God so loved the world that he gave his only Son, so that everyone who believes in him may not perish but may have eternal life." So, the birth of Jesus is part of how God concretely demonstrates his love for humanity.

In many ways, this book has been a reflection on a collection of stories that shows us God's love for humanity. God loved us by becoming one of us. When God became a human, he joined the human experience. It was from these common experiences that Jesus forged the foundation of his lasting, loving relationship with us.

If you've ever become friends with someone or dated someone, that relationship probably began with things you had in common. My wife and I started dating because we took Greek class together. Because I "needed" a study partner, we began to hang out as classmates. Then we spent time together as friends. Then we began to date. The more time we spent together, the more we shared common experiences and found out where we had common interests. These points of commonality became one of the foundations of our love. Conversely, people can also grow out of love when they stop sharing common experiences.

Christmas challenges us to be like Jesus. We are called to reach out to others. We can discover points of contact so that we can show them love just as Jesus showed us God's love. In fact, Jesus only gave us two commands—to love God and to love our neighbors (Matthew 22:34–40; Mark 12:28–34; Deuteronomy 6:5; Leviticus 19:18). If these are the two things we are supposed to do, then it is probably pretty important to understand how to do these things.

Possibly the most comprehensive definition of love comes from another famous passage in the Bible, 1 Corinthians 13, which begins by telling us that "Love is patient. Love is kind." If you are someone who

---

1. A good work that explores the Christian love ethic is: Furnish, *Love Command in the New Testament*.

likes definitions, then consider memorizing that chapter and making it an initial checklist on what defines love. If you are someone who thinks "actions speak louder than words," then consider reading the stories of Jesus and see how he treats others with compassion. Try to emulate his life, which followed the principles of putting others first and living a life of self-sacrifice (Mark 10:44–45).

To Be Used or Enjoyed?

Another approach to understanding love comes from Augustine. He talks about the difference between use and enjoyment. He says that love is only possible when we enjoy things. If we are using things, then we don't love them.

A good guideline for determining if you love someone or something is to ask yourself the following questions: Are you using that person or thing for another goal? Or are you enjoying that person or thing for their own sake? For example, do you go on a walk because you are trying to get some exercise for a healthy body? That would be using walking. Or do you take walks because you enjoy the time outside? That would be enjoying walking. Someone who loves to walk, walks for the sake of walking.

In terms of people, we can ask similar questions. Are we enjoying the people in our lives? Or do we use them because of the ways they make us feel? So, do we offer money to a homeless person because we feel guilty? Or do we give them money because we are concerned about their well-being? Do we spend time with someone because they make us feel happy? Or do we spend time with them because we enjoy their company?

This is where romantic love gets challenged by Augustine. Do we call something "love" because of how a person makes *us* feel? Do we love someone because they make *us* a better person? For Augustine, these things don't show a love for others. Instead, they reveal a narcissistic love for ourselves. True love involves simply enjoying another person's company. True love is not about us; it is about others. We may even find ourselves sacrificing our needs, wants, and desires on behalf of the other person when we truly love them.

We can also ask ourselves about our love for God. Do we love God because we don't want to go to hell? Is Jesus our eternal life insurance policy? Do we love God because we want to be in happy, healthy relationships? Do we love God in order to have better families, jobs, and futures?

Do we love God so that we feel better about ourselves? In other words, are we just using God to attain our own goals? Are we treating God like some magic genie who fulfills our desires?

What would it look like for us to pursue God just so that we could spend time with him? How do we learn just to enjoy God's company? What if we learned to uniquely express our love for God according to one of the five love languages? Could our prayer life be filled with words of affirmation? Maybe we could show our love through the gift giving of our tithes and offerings? Perhaps we enjoy acts of service? Do we spend quality time with God through meditation or spiritual retreats? Are we someone who feels the manifest presence of God in our lives?

Enjoy Your Christmas

So back to Christmas. Often Christmas gets used for many purposes. Retailers use Christmas to promote sales. Families can use Christmas to reconnect and show love for each other. Churches use Christmas to promote growth and attendance.

Is it possible for us to simply enjoy Christmas? Can we enjoy the celebration of the birth of Jesus? Can we enjoy the traditions? Can we enjoy the Bible stories? The real question is how do we go about enjoying Christmas for its own sake?

Part of the answer involves not making Christmas a means to another end. Christmas is not about what we can get out of the holiday. Instead, Christmas is about enjoying the story of God wanting to be with us. God wants to spend time with us, which is why he sent Jesus to this earth as a baby. Enjoying Christmas is about reminding ourselves what it means to have a relationship with God. Christmas is a reminder that God loves us.

Throughout this book we've taken some time to play with Christmas in order to learn how to enjoy Christmas for its own sake and to remember God's love. We've treated Christmas like a Lego set, finding the fun in taking the stories and traditions apart and putting them back together. In the process we've ruined a lot of things. For example, Jesus's birthday isn't December 31. Jesus's name is actually Joshua. There wasn't an inn. The magi weren't kings. Christmas isn't meant to be commercialized and used.

We've also rediscovered Jesus. We can find Jesus every time we look at the date and remember his birth. By saying his name, we declare that Yahweh saves. While Jesus was rejected from his family's guestroom, he welcomes us into his family. Jesus also invites us to join his mission of reconciling races and to be like the astrologers who found their place around his manger. By looking carefully at Christmas stories and traditions like these, we've been able to enjoy Christmas and rediscover Jesus.

Merry Christmas!

Reflection Questions

1. What do the days after the Christmas holiday look like for you? Are you the type of person who leaves your decorations up as long as possible, or do you quickly put them away? How does taking down our holiday decorations help us get ready for Christmas the following year? How has this book helped you get ready for the next Christmas?

2. How does the Christmas story show God's love for humanity? How does this love for humanity inspire you to love others? Are there things that you can find in common with others so that you can learn to show them love?

3. The 5 *Love Languages* are (1) words of affirmation, (2) gift giving and receiving, (3) quality time, (4) acts of service, and (5) physical touch. Which one of these would be your primary way of showing and receiving love? Can you identify the primary love languages of other significant people in your life like your family or friends? Knowing that we communicate love differently with others, are there ways that you can improve how you show love to others?

4. What is something that you enjoy doing? Can you explain the difference between using and enjoying something? Is it better to enjoy something?

5. What are some ways that we use Christmas? What are ways that we can learn to enjoy Christmas for its own sake?

6. The greatest command is to love God (Deuteronomy 6:5). Are we using God to attain our own goals, or do we love God and seek his goals? How do we learn just to enjoy God's company?

7. The second greatest command is to love our neighbor (Leviticus 19:18). How can we learn to enjoy people in our lives rather than using them to fulfill our needs?

8. Did this book ruin anything about Christmas that helped you rediscover Jesus?

Activity: Worship

This chapter has encouraged us to learn to enjoy things. Are you someone who enjoys Christmas music? Do you listen to it during the whole month of December? Christmas music and church services create natural reminders for worship. Worship is a feeling or expression of reverence and adoration for God. As we conclude our study on Christmas, what are ways that we can respond by worshiping God? What are the good things in our lives that we can offer praises to God? Do we feel disorientated by personal or communal problems that need to be lamented? Can our worship help reorientate us on God?

Appendix A

The Earliest Records Dating Jesus's Birth

The following are early testimonies to the birth of Jesus:[1]

- **Origen**, *Leviticus Homily* 8 (AD 185–254) rejects all Christmas celebrations stating only sinners celebrate birthdays.

- **Clement of Alexandria**, *Stromateis* 1.21.145–46 (AD 215) favors November 18 but also mentions April 19, 20, May 20, and January 6, 10.

- **Hippolytus**, *Commentary on Daniel* 4.23 (AD 203–204) may date Jesus's birth to April 2 (earliest manuscripts) but also includes a later interpolated date of December 25.

- **Sextus Julius Africanus**, *Chronology* 1 (Greek title: *Chronographiai*, AD 221) favors the annunciation on March 25, which implies Jesus's birthday on December 25.

- *On Computing the Paschal Feast* (Latin title: *De Pascha Computus*, AD 243) identifies March 28 with Jesus's birth.

- *De solstitiis et aequinoctiis* (late fourth century, at least after AD 274) calculates Jesus's birth on December 25 because it is fifteen months after John's conception (Luke 1:26, 39) and nine months after Jesus's conception and passion on March 25. This tractate was, for a period, incorrectly attributed to John Chrysostom.

- **Furius Dionysius Philocalus**, *Chronograph* (AD 336) records a date of December 25.

---

1. For a discussion of these texts, see Roll, *Towards the Origins of Christmas*, 77–87, 100–105, 117.

- **Gregory of Nazianzen,** *In theophaniam oratio* 38 (AD 381) claims to be the originator of the December 25 celebration in Constantinople.

- **John Chrysostom,** *In diem natalem* (AD 386–388) calculates the date to December 25 to encourage the Eastern church in Antioch to adopt the feast practices of the West.

- **Augustine,** *On the Trinity* 4.5 (AD 399–419) calculates December 25 as nine months after Jesus's conception and passion on March 25.

— Appendix B —

Advent Wreaths

I grew up opening Christmas presents on Christmas Eve. My parents made this decision for the very pragmatic reason that they had no desire to be woken up by loud, noisy, and excited children on Christmas morning. As kids, we were just excited to open our presents one day earlier than all of our friends!

Our Christmas Eve tradition involved having a nice supper, then attending our church's Christmas Eve service, and returning home to open Christmas presents. But before we would open our presents, mom would get out her homemade Advent wreath so that we could tell the story of Jesus as a family by reading verses and lighting candles.

Lighting the Advent candles is one of my favorite Christmas memories. However, if you ever had seen our wreath, you might be a bit embarrassed for us. Mom had assembled all the various parts from the local crafts supply store. The base was made of green Styrofoam in which she had poked fake evergreen branches and five candles—four red and one white.

To add to the effect, we used the same five candles each year. We preserved them by only lighting the candles for a few minutes before blowing them out. As time went on, the candles became slightly discolored and bent. They also managed to drip their wax over the evergreen base.

In addition, there were five yellow stars, which mom had cut out of construction paper. On the front of the star, she had typed an Old Testament verse, and on the back, she typed a New Testament verse. However, because this was long before computers, a few of the verses had typos that had been crossed out.

After I left for college, my mom tried to get rid of the old Advent wreath and replace it with a new one. But after over twenty years of use, my sister and I loudly protested. We kept using that old Advent wreath until it was in such bad shape that we had to replace it. But even this new Advent wreath still uses some of the fake evergreen branches from the original.

While the old wreath is ruined, our family has been able to enjoy new memories with a rebuilt wreath. I wanted to share with you the basic elements of our Advent celebration with the hope that it inspires and enriches your own family or community's celebration. The following is the collection of traditions and verses that my family uses each year to celebrate Christmas.

Elements of the Wreath

A traditional wreath is made of evergreens because these trees don't change color or lose their leaves in winter, which serve as a reminder of God's faithfulness to his people by granting them eternal life through Christ. The evergreens are arranged in a circle to remind people of God's unity and unbroken promises.

Wreaths consist of at least four candles—hope, peace, joy, and love. The flames remind us that Christ is the light of the world. These four candles are usually lit on the four Sundays prior to Christmas. The progressive lighting symbolizes the expectation of Christ's coming.

These four candles come in a variety of colors. Among Protestants, they may be red to represent Jesus's blood. Among Lutherans and Anglicans, they may also be blue to represent hope. For Catholics, three of the candles are purple to symbolize the repentance done in preparation for celebrating Jesus's birth. The third candle of joy is sometimes pink (or rose), since this color is a mixture of purple and white, symbolizing the joyous anticipation of the season.

Some wreaths include a fifth candle, which represents the gospel. This candle is usually placed at the center and is white to represent Christ, whose holiness makes people pure through his saving work.

There are many ways that families and churches can celebrate Advent together. Some churches follow their prescribed church calendars. Some families light a new candle each week in the morning or at dinner. Other families chose to light all the candles of the Advent wreath on Christmas Eve or Christmas Day.

There are a variety of Advent verse readings. The following verses are based on what my family reads each year.[1] The first verses are Old Testament messianic prophecies related to Christ's birth. For week one, Matthew 1:23 recounts the virgin birth and quotes Isaiah 7:14. The second week presents the angelic announcement of peace in Luke 2:14 as an allusion to Isaiah 9:6. For week three, Matthew 2:6 tells his audience that Jesus's birth in Bethlehem fulfills Micah 5:2. In week four, the story of the magi in Matthew 2:1–12 alludes to Isaiah 60:1–3. Finally, Jesus quotes from Isaiah 61:1–2 as his gospel message in Luke 4:18–19.

The second set of verses are from the New Testament. They progressively tell the Christmas story. Week one begins with the annunciation of Jesus's birth. Week two tells of the family's journey from Nazareth and Jesus's birth in Bethlehem. Week three relates the angelic announcement and shepherds' visit. Week four presents the coming of the magi. Week five concludes with a reminder of the gospel.

In addition, each set of verses is related to the week's advent theme. For the first week, the prophecy of the virgin birth gives hope. In week two, Jesus is called the prince of peace. The angels bring good tidings of great joy in week three. The fourth week recounts the coming of the magi to show God's love for the whole world. The final week relates the good news message.

First Candle: Hope

"Therefore the Lord himself will give you a sign: The virgin will conceive and give birth to a son, and will call him Immanuel" (Isaiah 7:14).

"In the sixth month the angel Gabriel was sent by God to a town in Galilee called Nazareth, to a virgin engaged to a man whose name was Joseph, of the house of David. The virgin's name was Mary . . . . The angel said to her, 'Do not be afraid, Mary, for you have found favor with God. And now, you will conceive in your womb and bear a son, and you will name him Jesus'" (Luke 1:26–27, 30–31).

---

1. The verses below are from the NIV.

Second Candle: Peace

"For to us a child is born, to us a son is given, and the government will be on his shoulders. And he will be called Wonderful Counselor, Mighty God, Everlasting Father, Prince of Peace" (Isaiah 9:6).

"In those days Caesar Augustus issued a decree that a census should be taken of the entire Roman world . . . . So Joseph also went up from the town of Nazareth in Galilee to Judea, to Bethlehem the town of David, because he belonged to the house and line of David. He went there to register with Mary, who was pledged to be married to him and was expecting a child. While they were there, the time came for the baby to be born, and she gave birth to her firstborn, a son. She wrapped him in cloths and placed him in a manger, because there was no guest room available for them" (Luke 2:1, 4–7).

Third Candle: Joy

"But you, Bethlehem Ephrathah, though you are small among the clans of Judah, out of you will come for me one who will be ruler over Israel, whose origins are from of old, from ancient times" (Micah 5:2).

"And there were shepherds living out in the fields nearby, keeping watch over their flocks at night. An angel of the Lord appeared to them, and the glory of the Lord shone around them, and they were terrified. But the angel said to them, 'Do not be afraid. I bring you good news that will cause great joy for all the people. Today in the town of David a Savior has been born to you; he is the Messiah, the Lord' . . . So they hurried off and found Mary and Joseph, and the baby, who was lying in the manger. When they had seen him, they spread the word concerning what had been told them about this child" (Luke 2:8–11, 16–17).

Fourth Candle: Love

"Arise, shine; for your light has come, and the glory of the Lord has risen upon you. For darkness shall cover the earth, and thick darkness the peoples; but the Lord will arise upon you, and his glory will appear over you. Nations shall come to your light, and kings to the brightness of your dawn" (Isaiah 60:1–3).

"After Jesus was born in Bethlehem in Judea, during the time of King Herod, Magi from the east came to Jerusalem . . . . When they saw the star, they were overjoyed. On coming to the house, they saw the child with his mother Mary, and they bowed down and worshiped him. Then they opened their treasures and presented him with gifts of gold, frankincense, and myrrh. And having been warned in a dream not to go back to Herod, they returned to their country by another route" (Matthew 2:1, 10–12).

Fifth Candle: Gospel

"The spirit of the Lord God is upon me, because the Lord has anointed me; he has sent me to bring good news to the oppressed, to bind up the brokenhearted, to proclaim liberty to the captives, and release to the prisoners; to proclaim the year of the Lord's favor" (Isaiah 61:1–2).

"For God so loved the world that he gave his one and only Son, that whoever believes in him shall not perish but have eternal life" (John 3:16).

Bibliography

Allers, Roger, and Rob Minkoff, dir. *The Lion King*. Burbank: Walt Disney Pictures, 1994.

Allison, Dale, Jr. *Constructing Jesus: Memory, Imagination, History*. Grand Rapids: Baker Academic, 2010.

Auld, William Muir. *Christmas Traditions*. Detroit: Gale Research, 1968.

Augustine, Saint. *On Christian Teaching*. Translated by R. P. H. Green. New York: Oxford University Press, 1997.

Bailey, Kenneth. "The Manger and the Inn: The Cultural Background of Luke 2:7." *Near East School of Theology Review* 2 (1979) 33–44.

———. *Jesus through Middle Eastern Eyes*. Downers Grove, IL: IVP Academic, 2008.

Barnett, James. *The American Christmas: A Study in National Culture*. New York: Macmillan, 1954.

Barnett, Paul. "ἀπογραφή and ἀπογράφεσθαι in Luke 2:1–5." *Expository Times* 85 (1973–1974) 377–80.

Barr, James. "'*Abbā* Isn't Daddy." *Journal of Theological Studies* 39 (1988) 28–47.

Bates, Matthew. *Gospel Allegiance: What Faith in Jesus Misses for Salvation*. Brazos, 2019.

Bauer, D. R. "Genealogy." In *Dictionary of Jesus and the Gospels* 2nd ed., edited by Joel Green et al., 299–302. Downers Grove, IL: InterVarsity, 2013.

Beasley-Murray, George R. *Jesus and the Kingdom of God*. Grand Rapids: Eerdmans, 1985.

Beegle, Dewey. "Moses (Person)." In *Anchor Bible Dictionary*, edited by David Noel Freedman, 4:909–18. New York: Doubleday, 1992.

Bokser, Baruch. "Unleavened Bread and Passover, Feasts of." In *Anchor Bible Dictionary*, edited by David Noel Freedman, 6:755–65. New York: Doubleday, 1992.

Borg, Marcus, and John Dominic Crossan. *The First Christmas: What the Gospels Really Teach about Jesus's Birth*. New York: Harper One, 2007.

Botte, Bernard. *Les origins de la Nöel et de l'Épiphanie*. Louvain: Mont César, 1932.

Box, George. "Gospel Narratives of the Nativity." *Zeitschrift für die neutestamentliche Wissenschaft* 6 (1905) 80–101.

Brennan, Chrisann. *The Bite in the Apple: A Memoir of My Life with Steve Jobs*. New York: St. Martin's, 2013.

Brown, Raymond. *The Birth of the Messiah*. New updated edition. New York: Doubleday, 1993.

———. *The Virginal Conception and Bodily Resurrection of Jesus*. New York: Paulist, 1973.

Bulmer-Thomas, Ivor. "The Star of Bethlehem—A New Explanation—Stationary Point of a Planet." *Quarterly Journal of the Royal Astronomical Society* 33 (1992) 363–74.

Chapman, Gary. *The 5 Love Languages: The Secret to Love that Lasts*. Chicago: Northfield, 1992.

Chester, Craig. "The Star of Bethlehem." *Imprimis* 25 (1996) 1–6.

Chupungco, Anscar, ed. *Liturgical Time and Space*. Collegeville, MN: Liturgical, 2000.

Clark, David, et al. "An Astronomical Re-Appraisal of the Star of Bethlehem—A Nova in 5 BC." *Quarterly Journal of the Royal Astronomical Society* 18 (1977) 443–49.

Collins, Ace. *Stories Behind the Best-Loved Songs of Christmas*. Grand Rapids: Zondervan, 2001.

Connell, M. F. "Epiphany, The Solemnity of." In *New Catholic Encyclopedia*, 5:293–95. Detroit: Gale, 2003.

Crump, William. "Advent." In *The Christmas Encyclopedia*, n.p. Jefferson, NC: McFarland, 2013.

———. "Christmas Day." In *The Christmas Encyclopedia*, n.p. Jefferson, NC: McFarland, 2013.

Declercq, Georges. "Dionysius Exiguus and the Introduction of the Christian Era." *Sacris Eruditi* 41 (2002) 165–246.

Delling, Gehard. "*Parthenos*." In *Theological Dictionary of New Testament Theology*, edited by Gerhard Kittel and Gerhard Friedrich, translated by Geoffrey Bromiley, 5:826–37. Grand Rapids: Eerdmans, 1964–1976.

Donfried, Karl. "Chronology, New Testament." In *Anchor Bible Dictionary*, edited by David Noel Freedman, 1:1011–22. New York: Doubleday, 1992.

Duchesne, Louis. *Origines du culte chrétien*. Paris: Thorin, 1889.

Elkind, Peter. "When Steve Jobs' Ex-girlfriend Asked Him to Pay $25 Million for His 'Dishonorable Behavior.'" *Fortune*, August 6, 2015. https://fortune.com/2015/08/06/steve-jobs-apple-girlfriend/.

Friesen, Steven. "Poverty in Pauline Studies." *Journal for the Study of the New Testament* 26 (2004) 323–61.

Furnish, Victor. *The Love Command in the New Testament*. Nashville: Abingdon, 1972.

Giblin, C. H. "Reflections on the Sign of the Manger." *Catholic Biblical Quarterly* 29 (1967) 87–101.

Gibson, A. G. "Nicholas of Myra, St." In *New Catholic Encyclopedia*, 10:377–78. Detroit: Gale, 2003.

Green, Joel. *Gospel of Luke*. New International Commentary on the New Testament. Grand Rapids: Eerdmans, 1997.

———. "Kingdom of God/Heaven." In *Dictionary of Jesus and the Gospels* 2nd ed., edited by Joel Green et al., 468–81. Downers Grove, IL: InterVarsity, 2013.

Gulevich, Tanya. "Santa Claus." In *Encyclopedia of Christmas and New Year's Celebrations*, 699–710. Detroit: Omnigraphics, 2003.

Hagner, Donald. *Matthew*. 2 vols. Word Biblical Commentary. Waco: Word, 1993–1995.

Hall, Robert. "Circumcision." In *Anchor Bible Dictionary*, edited by David Noel Freedman, 1:1025–31. New York: Doubleday, 1992.

Hobsbawm, Eric J., and Terence Ranger, eds. *The Invention of Tradition*. Cambridge: Cambridge University Press, 1983.

Hoehner, Harold, and Jeannine Brown. "Chronology." In *Dictionary of Jesus and the Gospels*, edited by Joel Green et al., 134–38. 2d ed. Downers Grove, IL: InterVarsity, 2013.

Horsley, Richard. *The Liberation of Christmas*. New York: Crossroad, 1989.

Horsley, Richard, and James Tracy. *Christmas Unwrapped: Consumerism, Christ, and Culture*. Harrisburg, PA: Trinity Press International, 2001.

Huffmann, D. S. "Genealogy." In *Dictionary of Jesus and the Gospels*, edited by Joel Green and Scot McKnight, 253–58. Downers Grove, IL: InterVarsity, 1992.

Humphreys, Colin. "The Star of Bethlehem—A Comet in 5 BC—and the Date of the Birth of Christ." *Quarterly Journal of the Royal Astronomical Society* 32 (1991) 389–407.

"Is Zwarte Piet Racism? Race Relations in the Netherlands." *The Economist*, November 2, 2013. https://www.economist.com/europe/2013/11/04/is-zwarte-piet-racism?fsrc =scn%2Ftw_ec%2Fis_zwarte_piet_racism.

Jeremias, Joachim. *Prayers of Jesus*. Translated by S. H. Hooke. London: SCM, 1972.

John Paul II. *The Word Made Flesh: The Meaning of the Christmas Season*. San Francisco: Harper & Row, 1985.

Johnson, Marshall. *The Purpose of Biblical Genealogies*. London: Cambridge University Press, 1969.

Joiner, Reggie. "Monday is Coming." Presented at the Orange Conference, Atlanta, April 28, 2016.

Jones, A. H. M. *Augustus*. New York: Norton, 1970.

Kanellos, Niolás. *Noche Buena: Hispanic American Christmas Stories*. New York: Oxford, 2000.

Keller, Seth. "The More Things Change." *New York Journal of American History* Winter (2004) 72–79.

Kelly, Joseph. *The Birth of Jesus according to the Gospels*. Collegeville, MN: Liturgical, 2004.

———. *The Origins of Christmas*. Rev. ed. Collegeville, MN: Liturgical, 2014.

Kidger, Mark. *The Star of Bethlehem: An Astronomer's View*. Princeton: Princeton University Press, 1999.

Knobloch, Frederick. "Adoption." In *Anchor Bible Dictionary*, edited by David Noel Freedman, 1:78–79. New York: Doubleday, 1992.

Lagrange, M.-J. "Où en est la question du recensement de Quirinius?" *Revue Biblique* (1911) 60–84.

Larson, Frederick. *The Star of Bethlehem*. Hammersmith: Atlantic Productions, 2007.

Le Donne, Anthony. *Historical Jesus: What Can We Know and How Can We Know It?* Grand Rapids: Eerdmans, 2011.

Longenecker, Bruce. "Exposing the Economic Middle: A Revised Economy Scale." *Journal for the Study of the New Testament* 31 (2009) 243–78.

Lord, Phil, and Christopher Miller, dir. *The Lego Movie*. Burbank: Warner Bros., 2014.

Malina, Bruce. "Magi." In *New Interpreter's Dictionary of the Bible*, edited by Katharine Sakenfeld et al., 3:766. 5 vols. Nashville: Abingdon, 2006–2009.

Martin, Ernest. *The Star of Bethlehem: The Star That Astonished the World*. Portland: ASK, 1991.

Martin, Ralph P. *A Hymn of Christ*. 3rd ed. Downers Grove, IL: InterVarsity, 1997.

Martin, Ralph P., and Carl N. Toney. *New Testament Foundations*. Eugene: Cascade, 2018.

McCaulley, Esau. *Reading While Black: African American Biblical Interpretation as an Exercise in Hope*. Downers Grove, IL: IVP Academic, 2020.

McKnight, Scot. *The King Jesus Gospel: Original Good News Revisited*. Rev. ed. Grand Rapids: Zondervan, 2016.

McNeil, Brenda Salter. *Roadmap to Reconciliation 2.0: Moving Communities into Unity, Wholeness and Justice*. Westmont: InterVarsity, 2020.

McWhorter, John. "Is 'Black Pete' Racist?" *Time*, December 3, 2013. https://ideas.time.com/2013/12/02/is-black-pete-racist/.

Meier, John. *A Marginal Jew: The Roots of the Problem and the Person*. New York: Doubleday, 1991.

Meyer, Ben. "Jesus (Person)." In *Anchor Bible Dictionary*, edited by David Noel Freedman, 3:773–96. New York: Doubleday, 1992.

Molnar, Michael. *The Star of Bethlehem: The Legacy of the Magi*. Updated ed. New Brunswick: Rutgers University Press, 2013.

Morehouse, A. J. "The Christmas Star as a Supernova in Aquila." *Journal of the Royal Astronomical Society of Canada* 72 (1978) 65–68.

Nicholl, Colin. *The Great Christ Comet: Revealing the True Star of Bethlehem*. Wheaton: Crossway, 2015.

―――. "What Is Wrong with Rick Larson's 'Star of Bethlehem' DVD Documentary." Union Foundation, 2007. www.uniontheology.org/resources/doctrine/jesus/what-is-wrong-with-rick-larsons-star-of-bethlehem-dvd-documentary.

Nissenbaum, Stephen. *The Battle for Christmas: A Social and Cultural History of Our Most Cherished Holiday*. New York: Alfred A. Knopft, 1997.

Nolland, John. *Luke*. 3 vols. Word Biblical Commentary. Dallas: Word, 1989–1993.

Nunn, Trevor, and John Caird, dir. *Les Misérables*. London: Royal Shakespeare Company, 1985.

O'Shea, W. J., and S. K. Roll. "Advent." In *New Catholic Encyclopedia*, 1:133–35. Detroit: Gale, 2003.

Pasquin, John, dir. *The Santa Clause*. Burbank: Walt Disney Pictures, 1994.

Pandey, Nandini. "Caesar's Comet, the Julian Star, and the Invention of Augustus." *Transactions of the American Philological Association* 143 (2013) 405–49.

Plummer, Alfred. *A Critical and Exegetical Commentary on the Gospel according to St. Luke*. International Critical Commentary. Edinburgh: T. & T. Clark, 1902.

Potter, D. S. "Augustus (Emperor)." In *Anchor Bible Dictionary*, edited by David Noel Freedman, 1:524–28. New York: Doubleday, 1992.

Powell, Mark Allan. "The Magi as Kings: An Adventure in Reader-Response Criticism." *Catholic Biblical Quarterly* 62 (2000) 459–80.

―――. "The Magi as Wise Men: Re-examining a Basic Supposition." *New Testament Studies* 46 (2000) 1–20.

Rah, Soon-Chan. *Prophetic Lament: A Call for Justice in Troubled Times*. Westmont: InterVarsity, 2015.

Ramsey, J. T., and A. L. Licht. *The Comet of 44 B.C. and Caesar's Funeral Games*. Atlanta: Scholars, 1997.

Ramsay, William. *The Bearing of Recent Discovery on the Trustworthiness of the New Testament*. 4th ed. London: Hodder & Stoughton, 1920.

Reckart, Timothy, dir. *The Star*. Culver City: Sony Pictures, 2017.

Richards, E. G. *Mapping Time: The Calendar and Its History*. Rev. ed. New York: Oxford University Press, 2000.

Roll, Susan. "Christmas and Its Cycle." In *New Catholic Encyclopedia*, 3:551–57. Detroit: Gale, 2003.

―――. *Toward the Origins of Christmas*. Kampen: Kok Pharos, 1995.

Sanders, Fred. *The Triune God*. Grand Rapids: Zondervan, 2017.

———. "We Actually Don't Need a Trinitarian Revival." *Christianity Today Online*. May 23, 2017. https://www.christianitytoday.com/ct/2017/may-web-only/we-dont-need-trinity-revival-fred-sanders.html.

Seuss, Dr. *How the Grinch Stole Christmas!* New York: Random House, 1957.

Schaff, Philip. *The Creeds of Christendom, with a History and Critical Notes.* 3 vols. New York: Harper & Brothers, 1878–90.

Schenck, K. "Gospel: Good News." In *Dictionary of Jesus and the Gospels* 2nd ed., edited by Joel Green et al., 342–45. Downers Grove, IL: InterVarsity, 2013.

Schmidt, Leigh. *Consumer Rites: The Buying and Selling of American Holidays.* Princeton: Princeton University Press, 1995.

Schneemelcher, Wilhelm, ed. *New Testament Apocrypha.* Translated and edited by Robert McL. Wilson. 2 vols. Rev. ed. Louisville: Westminster John Knox, 2003.

Seow, C. L. "God, Names of." In *New Interpreter's Dictionary of the Bible,* edited by Katharine Sakenfeld et al., 2:588–94. Nashville: Abingdon, 2006–2009.

Smith, C. "Christmas and Its Cycle." In *New Catholic Encyclopedia,* 3:655–60. McGraw-Hill: San Francisco, 1967.

Spielberg, Stephen, dir. *Jaws.* Universal City: Universal Pictures, 1975.

Strauss, D. F. *The Life of Jesus Critically Examined,* edited by P. C. Hodgson, translated by G. Elliot. London: SCM, 1972.

Steel, Duncan. *Marking Time: The Epic Quest to Invent the Perfect Calendar.* New York: Wiley, 2000.

Talbert, Charles. *Matthew.* Paideia. Grand Rapids: Baker Academic, 2010.

Talley, Thomas. *The Origins of the Liturgical Year.* New York: Pueblo, 1986.

Thurston, Bonnie. "Widow." In *New Interpreter's Dictionary of the Bible,* edited by Katharine Sakenfeld et al., 5:847. Nashville: Abingdon, 2006–2009.

Usener, Hermann. *Das Weihnachtsfest.* 1st ed. Bonn: Cohen, 1889.

van Kooten, George H., and Peter Barthel, eds. *The Star of Bethlehem and the Magi.* Themes in Biblical Narrative 19. Leiden: Brill, 2015.

Vancil, Jack. "Sheep, Shepherd." In *Anchor Bible Dictionary,* edited by David Noel Freedman, 5:1187–90. New York: Doubleday, 1992.

Vaughn, Andrew. "Carpenter." In *New Interpreter's Dictionary of the Bible,* edited by Katharine Sakenfeld et al., 1:570. Nashville: Abingdon, 2006–2009.

Wallace, Howard. "Eden, Garden of (Place)." In *Anchor Bible Dictionary,* edited by David Noel Freedman, 2:281–83. New York: Doubleday, 1992.

Walton, John. "עֲלוּמִים." In *New International Dictionary of Old Testament Theology and Exegesis,* edited by Willem A. Van Gemeren, 4:415–19. Grand Rapids: Zondervan, 1997.

Watts, John. *Isaiah.* 2 vols. Rev. ed. Word Biblical Commentary. Nashville: Thomas Nelson, 2005.

Wernecke, Herbert. *Christmas Customs around the World.* Philadelphia: Westminster, 1959.

Wildberger, Hans. *Isaiah 1–12.* Translated by T. H. Trapp. Biblischer Kommentar Altes Testament 10. Minneapolis: Augsburg, 1991.

Winn, Adam. "Son of God." In *Dictionary of Jesus and the Gospels* 2nd ed., edited by Joel Green et al., 886–94. Downers Grove, IL: InterVarsity, 2013.

———, ed. *An Introduction to Empire in the New Testament.* Atlanta: SBL, 2016.

Witherington Ben, III. *Matthew.* Smyth & Helwys Bible Commentary. Macon: Smyth & Helwys, 2006.

Witherington, Ben, III, and K. Yamazaki-Ransom. "Lord." In *Dictionary of Jesus and the Gospels* 2nd ed., edited by Joel Green et al., 526–35. Downers Grove, IL: InterVarsity, 2013.

Wright, N. T. *Jesus and the Victory of God.* Minneapolis: Fortress, 1996.

———. *New Testament and People of God.* Minneapolis: Fortress, 1992.

Yancey, George. *Beyond Racial Gridlock: Embracing Mutual Responsibility.* Downers Grove, IL: InterVarsity, 2009.

Ziesler, J. A. "Matthew and the Presence of Jesus." *Epworth Review* 11 (1984) 55–63, 90–97.

Subject Index

Author Index

Ancient Document Index

CPSIA information can be obtained
at www.ICGtesting.com
Printed in the USA
FSHW010644111121